Limits of Rightness

Limits of Rightness

Michael Krausz

ROWMAN & LITTLEFIELD PUBLISHERS, INC.
Lanham • Boulder • New York • Oxford

ROWMAN & LITTLEFIELD PUBLISHERS, INC.

Published in the United States of America
by Rowman & Littlefield Publishers, Inc.
4720 Boston Way, Lanham, Maryland 20706
http://www.rowmanlittlefield.com

12 Hid's Copse Road
Cumnor Hill, Oxford OX2 9JJ, England

British Library Cataloguing in Publication Information Available

Library of Congress Cataloging-in-Publication Data

Krausz, Michael.
    Limits of rightness / Michael Krausz.
        p. cm. — (Philosophy and the global context)
    Includes bibliographical references (p.) and index.
    ISBN 0-7425-1168-5 (alk. paper) — ISBN 0-7425-1169-3 (pbk. : alk. paper)
    1. Hermeneutics. 2. Realism. 3. Constructivism (Philosophy) I. Title. II. Series.

BD241 .K735 2000
121'.68—dc21   00-059053

Printed in the United States of America

∞™ The paper used in this publication meets the minimum requirements of American
National Standard for Information Sciences—Permanence of Paper for Printed Library
Materials, ANSI/NISO Z.39.48-1992.

For my mother, Susan Krausz, with love.

"Philosophy is an activity in which one creates the conceptual space in which one can live." —Sir Isaiah Berlin

Contents

Acknowledgments   ix

Introduction   1

1   Ideals of Interpretation: Singularism versus Multiplism   5

2   A Multiplist and an Example: Margolis and the Kiefer Paintings   19

3   That Which Is Interpreted   25

4   Realism and Constructivism   35

5   Toward a Constructive Realism   51

6   Constructive Realists (I): Harré   59

7   Constructive Realists (II): Harrison and Hanna, and Wallner   65

8   Constructive Realists (III): Putnam and Gupta   75

9   Constructive Realists (IV): Margolis   87

10 Questions about Indeterminacy and Identity   101

11 Aims of Interpretation   113

12 Two Soteriologies   123

13 Life Paths and Projects   137

14 Conclusion   149

Bibliography   157

Index   161

About the Author   169

Acknowledgments

This work has benefited from discussions with many colleagues and friends, and I thank them for their good counsel. They include Margaret Bent, Richard Benz, Sir Isaiah Berlin, Noël Carroll, Peter Caws, Ruth Chang, Deen Chatterjee, G. A. Cohen, David Crocker, the Dalai Lama, Rosemary Desjardins, William Dray, Susan Feagin, Stiv Fleishman, James Griffin, Lobsang Gyatso, Rom Harré, Charles Harvey, Lucas Introna, Deborah Knight, Tony Kostroman, Bruno Latour, Joseph Margolis, Bojana Mladenovich, Jitendra Mohanty, Alexander Nehamas, Robert Nozick, Derek Parfit, Srinivasa Rao, Joseph Raz, Samdhong Rinpoché, Ina Rösing, Alan Ryan, Geshe Ngawang Samten, Simon Saunders, Kenneth Schmitz, Amartya Sen, Swami Shyam, Robert Stecker, Paul Thom, Laurence Thomas, J. D. Trout, and Joseph Wagner. Those who read the whole manuscript at various stages and offered extensive suggestions include Jacques Catudal, Jay Garfield, Chhanda Gupta, Bernard Harrison, Christine Koggel, Michael McKenna, and Paul Snowden. I especially thank them for their care and helpful suggestions. Finally, and mostly, I thank my wife, Connie Costigan, for her enduring love and support.

Introduction

One's conduct of inquiry is largely shaped by one's answer to the question whether there must always be a single admissible interpretation. Might there be more than one admissible interpretation, and under what conditions would they obtain? And under what conditions would it be inappropriate to speak of either one or more admissible interpretation? More fully, my questions come in clusters:

- Must there be a single right interpretation for such cultural entities as works of art, literature, music, or other cultural phenomena? Can opposing interpretations be jointly defended?
- What bearing does the aim of interpretation have on the range of ideally admissible interpretations? Does interpretation seek one or more aims?
- Does interpretive activity affect the nature and identity of that which is interpreted? What sorts of ontological entanglements are involved in interpretive activity? What is the relation between the indeterminacy of interpreted objects and their multiple interpretability?
- Under what conditions does the very idea of rightness or admissibility apply? For what sorts of phenomena are there no right interpretations, whether one or more?
- How do issues concerning the singularity or multiplicity of admissible interpretations bear on the singularity or multiplicity of life paths and projects?

Singularism is the view that that which is interpreted should always answer to one and only one ideally admissible interpretation. It holds that there should be a one–one match between that which is interpreted and its interpretation. In contrast, multiplism is the view that that which is interpreted need not always answer to one and only one fully congruent ideally

1

admissible interpretation. That is, there may be a one–many match between that which is interpreted and its interpretations, and the interpretations may be opposed but not exclusive.

By defining singularism and multiplism in terms of admissibility rather than rightness, I mean to avoid the ring of singularity that the word *rightness* sometimes misleadingly carries. That ring is by no means necessary, as evidenced by such remarks as "there may be more that one 'right' answer." I do not define rightness in terms of singularism. Doing so would beg the question to be pursued here. So to avoid confusion I speak of admissibility.

Multiplism requires that competing interpretations address the *same* thing. Where different interpretations address different things, no multiplism obtains. Rather, a philosophically innocuous "pluralism" obtains. Further, there are interesting cases that do not answer to the interpretive ideals of singularism *or* multiplism. Those cases include those where that which is interpreted cannot be clearly delineated as to number, where, that is, it cannot be determined whether one is speaking of one object of interpretation or where conflicting interpretations address themselves to a *common* object of interpretation. Neither singularism nor multiplism applies where interpretations themselves cannot be delineated as to number. They also don't apply where that which is interpreted is taken to be ineffable.

Numerous grounds have been offered for multiplism. First, multiplism has been thought to be secured by an "imputationist" or "determinability" view of interpretation (notably advanced by Joseph Margolis), according to which interpretive activity has the power to impute properties to, and thereby change, that which is interpreted. I shall consider whether imputationism is coherently adoptable, and whether (if imputationism be granted in pertinent cases) it indeed entails multiplism. I shall find that imputationism does not uniquely ground multiplism over singularism, since imputationism is also compatible with singularism.

Second, multiplism sometimes has been thought to be secured by the indeterminacy of that which is interpreted. That is, more than one interpretation has been taken to be admissible on the condition that its indeterminacy allows it to answer to more than one interpretation. I shall find that indeterminacy is not sufficient for multiplism. Of indeterminate objects of interpretation it might be best to say we do not know whether they answer to one or more than one ideally admissible interpretation.

Third, multiplism has been thought to be secured by the thought that that which is interpreted answers to distinct aims of interpretation. That is, different interpretations are admissible if they satisfy different aims of interpretation. So, if an interpretation satisfies the general aim of elucidation of that which is interpreted, for example, and if another interpretation satisfies the general aim of edification (whether personal as in vocational necessities on the one hand, or social and historical as in cultural or historical reconciliation on the other hand), a multiplicity of interpretations would be admissible. I shall consider whether there are one or more aims of interpretation, and whether it would be better to regard such concerns as edification as nonessential to *interpretation*. Further, I shall consider whether the assignment of any aim essential to interpretation runs counter to the general antiessentialist stance of this essay.

We should be clear about the relation between ideals of interpretation and certain ontological theories of pertinent objects of interpretation. In my book, *Rightness and Reasons*,[1] I suggest that singularism and multiplism are both compatible with the ontologies of realism and constructivism. The singularist–realist position is orthodox and it affirms, simply, that that which is interpreted is interpretation-independent and that there is one ideal interpretation of it, or at least one should behave as if there is one. The view arises primarily with ordinary middle-size objects in mind. The other orthodox position is multiplist–constructivist. It holds that that which is interpreted is interpretation-dependent and that there may be more than one ideally admissible interpretation of it, or at least one should behave as if there may be more than one. This orthodox position is usually embraced with cultural entities in mind. (When I call a combined position orthodox I mean to flag a tendency of association.) Heterodox possibilities are singularist–constructivist and multiplist–realist. The singularist–constructivist concedes that the object of interpretation is constructed (by a creator or by his or her culture) and with sufficiently thick description of the conditions of its construction there must be convergence toward a single admissible interpretation. Finally, the multiplist–realist holds that objects of interpretation are themselves interpretation-independent, but that incongruent interpretations are ideally admissible of them.

I have argued that the positions combined in these orthodox and heterodox combinations are *not necessary* because each of the combinations is coherently adoptable. Consequently, the contest between singularism and multiplism is *detachable* from the contest between realism and constructivism. In this essay I shall add that the contest between singularism and multiplism is also detachable from a range of other ontologies that I collect under the irenic heading of "constructive realism." I offer a ramified mapping of the ontological field, now disallowing that realism and constructivism are exhaustive. In this inventory I include the ontologies of Paul Thom, Rom Harré, Bernard Harrison and Patricia Hanna, Fritz Wallner, Hilary Putnam, Chhanda Gupta, and Joseph Margolis. I find that even according to the ramified mapping of the ontological field, the contest between singularism and multiplism still remains detachable from pertinent ontologies. None of the ontologies in our ramified inventory (which can never be exhaustive) uniquely entails either singularism or multiplism. While, in the course of discussion of these ontologies, I express favor for one or another, the overall argument for the detachability thesis does not depend upon it. And the detachability thesis does not depend upon an essentialist understanding of ontology.

Further, even if ideality is detachable from the ontological theories considered, one should not conclude that *no broadly metaphysical* issues are pertinent in discussions about interpretation. Indeed, the very distinction between that which is interpreted and its interpretations has metaphysical import. And neither singularism nor multiplism is formulable without that distinction. Further, in their existential versions (as I shall say), singularism and multiplism make existential claims about the *existence* of a single or multiple admissible interpretations.

In addition, the intentionality of that which is interpreted also involves metaphysical considerations. Intentionality concerns the cultural settings—rules, norms, and the like—in terms of which any cultural entity must be made intelligible. The thicker the intentional context, the narrower the range of admissible interpretations may become. So if we include claims of existence and intentionality as metaphysical, we may say that metaphysics is generally pertinent to interpretive concerns. There are metaphysical entanglements in the discussion about interpretation. But one should be clear where those entanglements lie.

The detachability question is significant, for it allows us to see what is and what is not entailed by singularism and multiplism. And it allows us to see what is and what is not entailed by realism, constructivism, or constructive realism. Now, the detachability thesis might serve those with different interests. It might serve those who see interpretative ideals as being held hostage by certain ontologies. It might serve those who see certain ontologies as being held hostage by certain interpretive ideals. It might even serve those who see the detachment as a preliminary step in receding the issues of both interpretive ideals and ontology in the service of yet other interests.

Finally, I extend the notion of ideals of interpretation of pertinent *objects* to ideals of *life paths and projects*. In that context I develop the ideas of directional singularism and directional multiplism. Directional singularism is the view that for a given person there is one admissible life path, and directional multiplism is the view that for a given person there may be more than one admissible life path. In the course of discussions of the views of Martha Nussbaum and David Norton I develop the idea of directional multiplism from an antiessentialist view of human nature.

NOTE

1. Michael Krausz, *Rightness and Reasons: Interpretation in Cultural Practices* (Ithaca, N.Y.: Cornell University Press, 1993).

Chapter One

Ideals of Interpretation: Singularism versus Multiplism

Distinctions and Strategies

SINGULARISM AND MULTIPLISM

Let us distinguish between two ideals of interpretation. The singularist ideal holds that for any object of interpretation, there must be one and only one ideally admissible interpretation of it. All objects of interpretation answer to this condition. In contrast, the multiplist ideal holds that some objects of interpretation may answer to more than one (opposed but not exclusive) ideally admissible interpretation of them. The multiplist allows, therefore, that *some* objects of interpretation answer to one admissible interpretation. In this regard singularism and multiplism are asymmetrical. While singularism claims that *all* objects of interpretation are singularly interpretable, multiplism holds that *some* objects of interpretation may answer to more than one admissible interpretation. The multiplist allows that a particular object of interpretation may answer to *one or more* admissible interpretation.

The singularist ideal is compatible with two versions: (a) the *existential* version holds that for pertinent objects there *is* one and only one admissible interpretation of it; and (b) the *regulative* version holds that an interpreter should assume and *act in accord* with the assumption that there is only one such interpretation. The regulative version does not commit one to the existential version.

Alexander Nehamas, for example, offers his singularist view in its regulative version.[1] That is, he distinguishes between *pursuing* the single right interpretation from *asserting* that there actually is a single right interpretation. He notes that the pursuit of a posited single right interpretation does not commit him to the claim that there actually is one such interpretation. The question arises whether, for a given object of interpretation, it would be reasonable to pursue a singularist ideal were one to hold that it would not or could not actually answer to a singularist condition. Would such a stance not be quixotic? If one believed that there were no one single admissible interpretation, should one nevertheless conduct one's inquiry as if there were? Nehamas seems unconcerned with this question, since his central focus is on the conduct of inquiry independent of the question whether certain objects of interpretation could actually answer to a singularist condition. In any event, the hypothetical posture departs from the assertoric posture concerning the one and only one admissible interpretation.

The singularist would not allow conjoining contradictory interpretations in one comprehensive interpretation. Yet the multiplist would allow more than one interpretation as ideally admissible if they were opposed but not exclusive. If they were exclusive and one of the exclusive interpretations were admissible, the other(s) would be rejected as inadmissible. Two incommensurable interpretations that address a common object of interpretation, for example, may be conjoined without violating the law of noncontradiction. They may be taken to oppose each other but need not be exclusive.

"VIOLENCE" TO PRACTICES:
MUTATION WITHOUT MUTILATION

A multiplist might say that the imposition of singularism in all cases would "do violence" to certain practices. But, in accord with an antiessentialist attitude (which I shall develop in chapters 11 and 13), all that should be meant by any such an idiom as "doing violence" would concern mutation of a condition's historically received character rather than mutilation of a presumed inherent and invariant essence. Accordingly, when speaking nonessentialistically, for the multiplist to say that violence might be done to a practice by forcing singularism would only be to say that it is not in keeping with the received or inherited practice. This nonessentialist attitude allows that it is an empirical matter whether a practice has such and such a character. That is a matter that bears on its historically constituted and contingently revisable nature. In accordance with such an antiessentialism, a multiplist might heed the warning of Bimal Matilal when he remarks, "Once we give up the 'essentialist's' dogma, we would find it natural to talk about not mutilation or destruction but mutation and change."[2]

MULTIPLISM VERSUS CRITICAL PLURALISM

The distinction between singularism and multiplism might appear to be tantamount to the distinction between what has sometimes been called critical monism and critical pluralism. But it is not. Nehamas, for example, embraces the position that he calls "critical monism," and that *is* equivalent to "singularism," namely, in the existential version, for any object of interpretation there is a single admissible interpretation of it. Or in the regulative version, for any object of interpretation one should conduct one's inquiry as if there is a single admissible interpretation of it.[3]

But "critical pluralism" is not equivalent to "multiplism." Critical pluralism is the view that for some object of interpretation there is more than one ideally admissible interpretation of it and these admissible interpretations are *equally preferable*. Multiplism denies this last claim of critical pluralism. Multiplism holds that, among the multiple ideally admissible interpretations, there may be good reasons for preferring one or some to others. Admissible interpretations need not be equally preferable, and good reasons can be provided for such preferences.

Good reasons for preferences among admissible interpretations may be offered while it remains the case that such reasons are not strong enough to unseat as inadmissible those interpretations that are regarded as less preferred. They still remain admissible.[4] Again, the point of adopting the nomenclature of singularism/multiplism over that of critical monism/critical pluralism is to allow for good reasons for one's preferred interpretations. In multiplist cases, such reasons should not be so strong as to unseat all alternatives as inadmissible. If they were, singularism would result.

One might object that the notion of good reasons should be reserved for those reasons which show that of numerous possibilities one should exclusively adopt one over the others. That is, if reasons are good, they will be grounds for holding that one possibility is exclusively better than the others. And, if "good reasons" are weaker than that, they are not good reasons. But why make such a demand of good reasons? "Preference-warranting reasons" explicate why one reasonably embraces the option one does. They offer a ramified account of one's reasonable preferences. To require that good reason giving must issue in a single admissible interpretation is to question beggingly stipulate the function of good reason giving. So seen, inconclusive reason giving is no second best.

SINGULARISM AND RATIONALITY

One might hold that singularism is constitutive of rationality itself, that rationality and singularism are conceptually linked. Whether or not such a suggestion is offered in an essentialist or an antiessentialist spirit, there is no need to make such a conceptual linkage. One should not beg the question by defining rationality in terms of singularism. That having been said, it is all right to recommend the softer methodological procedure that holds that where pertinent, one should seek to narrow the range of admissible interpretations. Such a softer suggestion is distinct from the thought that one should *always* press for the singularist ideal because it is in the nature of rationality as such. The *narrowing* of the range of admissibility may well accord with ideals of rational practices. But the degree of convergence (full or partial) should be guided more by the natures of the objects of interpretation in their interpretive contexts rather than by a commitment to a postulated ideal of full convergence.

The range of admissible interpretations may be narrowed by providing thick descriptions of pertinent interpretive contexts. The thickening of descriptions of pertinent contexts may narrow the range of admissibility. Yet, whether or not such thickening succeeds in narrowing the range to a limit of one, such a procedure remains distinct from the singularist claim that, for the pertinent case, there is or should be only one ideally admissible interpretation. Put otherwise, thickening the description of a pertinent context is a reasonable procedure. Yet it is distinct from the claim that there is (or one should behave as if there is) one ideally admissible interpretation.

THE PROGRESS ARGUMENT

A further argument for singularism concerns the idea of progress. Nehamas assumes that progress from one interpretation to another requires that one posit that there is a single final interpretation, one that functions as an ideal to be approached. It is a working assumption on the basis of which we compare one interpretation to another. One needs to posit that at the end of inquiry there is an asymptote of one single correct interpretation. Whether or not there is a single correct interpretation (existential version), we should posit that there is one, and that one is aiming toward it (regulative version). But Nehamas's recommendation (even the regulative one) rests upon a logical error. To say that Y is better than X does not require positing either that there is an end of inquiry, or that at such an end there is an asymptote that is singularist. Critical comparison between two interpretations does not require the posit that there be one finally and conclusively correct interpretation. Nehamas fails to see that a multiplist may agree that interpretation Y is better than X without at the same time embracing the thought that such a judgment depends upon holding that interpretation Y more closely approximates the singular ideal limit. To say that interpretation Y is better than interpretation X does not mandate singularism. Progressivism does not entail singularism. The rejection of inadmissible interpretations can be effected by the multiplist just as strongly as by the singularist. The multiplist may rule out inadmissible interpretations while progressing toward an asymptote that itself accommodates more than one ideally admissible interpretation. Multiplism does accommodate progressivism. And, again, at the asymptote one may have good reasons for one's preferences yet such reasons not be so strong as to rule out all but one interpretation as admissible.

ALL THE TEXT'S FEATURES

Nehamas's remarks in support of singularism are as telling against singularism as they are against multiplism. He says:

> The critical monism [or singularism] which I advocate is a regulative ideal and identifies the meaning of a text with whatever is specified by that text's ideal interpretation. Such an interpretation would account for all of the text's features, though we can never reach it since it is unlikely that we can even understand what it is to speak of "all the features" of anything. What we have (and that is what we need) is the notion of one interpretation answering more questions about a text than another and thus being closer to that hypothetical ideal which would answer all questions.[5]

Nehamas is right to say that "it is unlikely that we can even understand what it is to speak of 'all the features' of anything." But the same point can be pressed with respect to the ideal interpretation's answering "all questions." How does Nehamas propose to enumerate all the questions that might be posed of anything? The number of something's features as well as the questions to which it might be subjected are not denumerable.

More fully, the singularist may press his or her point along the following lines. Whenever it appears that multiplism obtains, not enough questions have been asked. By filling in pertinent questions and by thickening the description of the context, it will emerge that there is one and only one fully admissible way to answer the question. In other words, multiplism masks the fact that not enough questions have been asked. Further, the singularist may concede that while the intentions of a creator may not be definitive (since his or her intentions may be indeterminate, or ambiguous or the like), and while the object of interpretation may be emergent in that some of its properties were unintended, the *concerns* of the artist may be sufficiently rich to converge upon a single right interpretation. Yet it remains an open question whether the perpetual refinement of questions and the thickening of contextual descriptions will give out before full convergence to a single interpretation.

THE END OF INQUIRY

Notice that the argument against "all the features" or "all the questions" cuts as much against multiplism as it does against singularism, at least in unqualified formulations. For the argument cuts against the very idea of an end of inquiry, of which singularism and multiplism are parasitic. Without some coherent idea of an end of inquiry, neither ideal would be coherently adoptable. But the idea of an end of inquiry remains serviceable only if it is not understood in terms of "all features" being accommodated or "all questions" answered. That is, the idea of an end of inquiry should be softened so as to understand an ideal in real time or pragmatic terms wherein informed practitioners may agree that all pertinent evidence or argumentation is available to make a suitably informed determination as to whether a given object of interpretation answers to one or more than one interpretation. That is, pertinent ideals should be understood within provisional, unfolding, and changing interpretive conditions.

A LIBERAL SINGULARISM AND A LIBERAL MULTIPLISM

A singularist might urge that there is a single admissible interpretation (or one should behave as if there is), but at the same time encourage the pursuit of alternative interpretations because they are interesting or illuminating, or because doing so is healthy for critical discourse in general.[6] This suggestion allows inadmissible interpretations to remain on the table, so to say. Yet this "liberal singularism" keeps singularism intact. More fully, on the liberal singularist view there must be a single admissible interpretation (or one should behave as if there is one), but the entertainment of alternative interpretations should be encouraged. It is in the interest of interpretative practices generally to encourage such alternative interpretations. For example, a singularist with respect to musical interpretation, holding that there is only one admissible interpretation for a given work of music, may encourage alternative interpretations. This liberal singularist view may be understood in terms of a distinction between *admissibility* and *encouragement*. Accordingly and perhaps ironically, inadmissibility should not carry discouragement with it.

Even the entertainment of inadmissible interpretations may be encouraged with the thought that with a greater number of interpretations on the table, admissible or inadmissible, one has a wider field of interpretive resources. So understood, the distinction between admissibility and encouragement may be deployed by either the singularist or the multiplist.

A liberal multiplist, on the other hand, may hold that, for a pertinent case, there is no conclusive standard or sufficiently thick contextual description to mandate singularism. But as a regulative matter it is useful to adopt singularism as a guiding principle, not so much in anticipation that a singularist condition will be achieved in real time terms but rather that it will motivate the search for further standards or thicker contextual descriptions that, in any event, will provide for at least a sharper understanding of the case and may narrow the range of admissible interpretations.

SINGULARISM AND FALLIBILISM

Singularism should not be confused with infallibilism. A singularist might well affirm that there is only one ideally admissible interpretation of a pertinent object (or behave as if there is one). But such a claim does not entail that the singularist is in possession of such an interpretation, or indeed that he or she has a methodology for identifying which of the candidate interpretations is the singularly admissible one. Singularism does not commit one to the view that any one interpretation embraced at a given time cannot, in light of criticism, be substituted by a better one. Singularism is altogether compatible with fallibilism.

MULTIPLISM AND RICHNESS

A cultural object is sometimes said to be rich, that is, upon repeated readings or viewings or hearings one "reads" or "sees" or "hears" more and more in it. Such works are sometimes said to stand the test of time. Notice that such a notion of richness does not mandate multiplism, for one could read or see or hear more and more, still on the condition that at the limit there is one most rich admissible reading or viewing or listening or admissible interpretation. The fact that one does not actually come to the limit does not inhibit the thought that at the limit there is one most rich reading or viewing or hearing or interpretation.

MULTIPLISM AND THE CULTURAL

Multiplism is no criterion of the cultural, for there are interesting cultural cases that do answer to the singularist condition. David Norton, for example, misleadingly sets out

> to show that the mutiplism . . . [Krausz] demonstrates is a definitive condition of all cultural objects-of-interpretation by any viable meaning of "cultural." [7]

Norton says further that

> my intention is to show that on any viable meaning of the term, "culture" entails multiplism, and therefore that multiplism is the epistemic condition of all objects-of-interpretation that are properly termed "cultural." [8]

Norton emphasizes his point that for *any* cultural object there must be more than one admissible interpretation of it when he says:

> whatever is not susceptible of irreducibly multiple alternative admissible interpretations is not a cultural object-of-interpretation. For example: if Shakespeare had successfully limited the admissible interpretations of *Hamlet* to one, then *Hamlet* would not be a cultural object-of-interpretation. And if objects of inquiry in the physical sciences are properly classed as cultural, it is because they are susceptible of alternative admissible interpretations, as Thomas Kuhn has famously argued in his contention for multiple paradigms of interpretation. [9]

Now, even if one could show that, of all the contending interpretations of *Hamlet*, there is one and only one interpretation that finally stands as admissible, that should not be taken as grounds that *Hamlet* is no cultural achievement. *Hamlet* is a cultural achievement par excellence, whether or not interpreters succeed in settling upon one or more admissible interpretations of it. Indeed, it is for this sort of reason that multiplism allows that certain singularist conditions might obtain. Further, it is hasty on Norton's part to say that Kuhn's thesis confers the status of the cultural on the physical sciences "because they are susceptible of alternative admissible interpretations." Kuhn in fact couples his thesis of the plurality or the alternativity of paradigms (which Norton reads as interpretations) with the further thesis that for each paradigm there comes into existence another "world" to which such paradigms address themselves. So understood, one might regard Kuhn as having provided an example of a singularist rather than a multiplist condition. That is, from a condition that one might first construe as multiplist—where different paradigms are taken to address the same thing—separate things are in fact addressed. This "pluralizing" maneuver, as I call it, results in a singularist condition. That is, if two paradigms address two separate worlds, the singularist condition is installed. There is a one–one relation between an interpretation and that which is interpreted. If Kuhn means to regard science as a cultural achievement it should not, as Norton says, be "because they [scientific objects of interpretation] are susceptible of alternative admissible interpretations." We should not go so far as Norton does to disallow that cultural objects may answer to a singularist condition. It would have been better if Norton had softened his claim to the effect that multiplism is perhaps *characteristic* rather than *definitive* of the cultural.

SINGULARIST AND MULTIPLIST STRATEGIES

Both singularist and multiplist conditions require that objects of interpretation and interpretations themselves be countable. Yet where objects of interpretation and interpretations may be variously counted, distinct strategies may be deployed by proponents of singularism and multiplism. When confronted with an object of interpretation that initially appears to answer to two or more interpretations, the singularist might attempt to install the singularist condition by *pluralizing* the object of interpretation. (Here "object of interpretation" means "intentional object" or "object as represented" as we shall see in chapters 2 and 3.) That is, the object of interpretation may be reconfigured so that there should result two or more distinct objects of interpretation. And for each of those reconfigured objects of interpretation there would result one and only one interpretation of it. Consider such a pluralizing maneuver in the case of Van Gogh's *Potato Eaters*. The multiplist may urge several competing interpretations of it. He or she may, for example, offer formalist, psychoanalytic, Marxist, feminist, or other interpretations of it. The singularist might counter by attempting to pluralize the object of interpretation by saying that these interpretations really are not interpretations of the same thing. In fine, they are interpretations of different objects of interpretation. Consequently, what the feminist takes as his or her object of interpretation differs from what the Marxist takes as his or her object of interpretation, notwithstanding the fact that such objects of interpretation may be embodied in the same physical canvas. In turn, the multiplist may counter by suggesting that always to invoke this pluralizing maneuver is misplaced. Indeed, the multiplist may urge that sometimes one should deploy the contrary strategy of *aggregating* objects of interpretation, where two or more objects of interpretation should be aggregated into one. Feminist and Marxist objects of interpretation should be aggregated into a feminist–Marxist one.

Further, the strategies of pluralizing or aggregating objects of interpretation find their analogs in corresponding strategies of pluralizing or aggregating interpretations themselves. That is, confronting a multiplist condition, a singularist may seek to aggregate two or more interpretations into one in order to install a singularist condition. For example, a Marxist and a feminist interpretation of the *Potato Eaters*, taken separately, may initially be taken to exemplify a multiplist condition. But the singularist might bring these together as one Marxist–feminist interpretation, claiming that the object of interpretation answers to that one aggregated interpretation. Or, in order to install a multiplist condition, a multiplist may pluralize a given interpretation (from a Marxist–feminist one to a Marxist one and a feminist one). No general rule suggests itself for determining when such maneuvers should be invoked.

INTENTIONAL OBJECTS OF INTERPRETATION

The feasibility of deploying the pluralizing or the aggregating strategies of objects of interpretation (whether in the service of singularists or multiplists) depends upon the sort of object it is. The mentioned strategies seem inapplicable for mere middle-sized objects as usually construed. Yet if as objects of interpretation we consider *intentional objects* the situation looks rather different. An intentional object is an object of attention, and its nature differs from mere middle-sized objects as such. Intentional objects are objects endowed with meaning or significance within a field of cultural codes and norms. They are *objects-as-represented* within a framework of cultural representation. Of intentionality Jitendra Mohanty says:

> Intentionality . . . is not mere directedness to a world, but interpretive of the world. It not only has its own content, it confers meaning on its object, so that its object is presented as having that meaning for it. [It is] . . . constitutive of the sense or senses of the world.[10]

In aggregating or pluralizing different intentional objects of interpretation, interpreters may take as salient (or as meaningful) different aspects of a common thing and accordingly offer interpretations of the resultant *intentionalized* object of interpretation. For example, a feminist may take certain aspects of the *Potato Eaters* as salient (say, the glance of the central female figure unresponded to by her male counterpart), in contrast to a religious interpretation which may take as salient the crucifix in the painting's background or the flooding light from the overhead lantern. These sets of aspects would have variously been taken as salient and accordingly would give rise to different intentional objects, which, in turn, invite different interpretations. At the same time, in order to say, as one might, that they are different interpretations of the same work, one would need to assume some *common grounding*. If one does not assume as much, the sets of aspects made salient would give rise to different objects of interpretation, and no conflict between interpretations would obtain. How, then, should we understand such common grounding? Realists, constructivists, and constructive realists provide different answers. We shall consider their answers in the next chapters.

For the moment we should note that intentionality concerns the intelligibility of a cultural entity as understood within a form of life or *lebenswelt*. It concerns a social setting as distinguished from an individual setting. Correspondingly, we may distinguish social intentionality from individual intentions. For example, when we distinguish a twitch from a wink we do so at the individual level as regards the intentions of an individual who might be interested in communicating a message thereby. But that message to begin with is intelligible within a socially intentional setting of norms, procedures, or shared values.

Typically, social intentionality restricts what is socially admissible, and thus it provides a ground for objectivity. But characteristically it is not sufficiently thick to mandate singularism, though singularism is consistent with it. Thus, while social intentionality provides objectivity in a broad sense, it is compatible with either singularism or multiplism.

AMBIGUOUS INTERPRETATIONS AND THEIR OBJECTS

Our central concern is with the singularity or multiplicity of interpretations with respect to a given object of interpretation. Note that an interpretation may be ambiguous in such a way that according to one of its "meanings" it may address one object of interpretation, and according to another meaning it may address a different object of interpretation. That is, a given interpretation may be ambiguous in such a way that according to one meaning it addresses one object, and according to another meaning it addresses a distinct object. In such a case, the ambiguous interpretation may point to distinctly separable sets of relations.

"ONTOLOGY" AND "METAPHYSICS"

In speaking of the detachability of ontology from ideality, I speak of "ontology" as a shorthand for realism, constructivism, or constructive realism. That narrow usage of "ontology" allows us to affirm that there is a larger "metaphysical" context that is implicated in the very idea of singularism and multiplism. That context includes the existential claims made by singularism and multiplism as well as the intentional considerations that help make particular objects of interpretation and interpretations intelligible. I use "metaphysics" as a more general term to include (not exclusively) pertinent existential claims and intentionality.

ALTERNATIVITY

Representative ontologies characteristically carry a rider that I call the rider of alternativity. It is sometimes thought that the rider of alternativity entails multiplism. But it does not. The rider of alternativity remarks that there is a multiplicity of taxonomic classifications, systems of counting, conceptual schemes, or the like. Now remember that multiplism holds that a given *single* object of interpretation is multiply and incongruently interpretable. Pluralism holds that different interpretations apply to *different* objects of interpretation. (Pluralism is really a version of singularism.) Accordingly, the fact of alternativity is characteristically taken to amount to the view that such classifications, schemes, or the like *address a common object*, and it is in virtue of their doing so that they are thought to be alternative ways of accounting for the *same thing*. But in the representative ontologies I shall consider *the slide from alternativity to commonality is characisticaly unsupported*. Put otherwise, alternativity alone is compatible with either multiplism or singularism (or pluralism).

Putnam, for example, holds that there are alternative ways of counting. Harré holds that there are diverse ways that an object may be "afforded." Margolis holds that different interpretations may impute objects differently, and Thom holds that the "further object" may be represented differently. Each of these ontologies affirms alternativity in that they take the alternativity of pertinent schemes as a datum. Yet given such alternativity alone, it remains open whether there is one thing that is being counted or afforded or imputed or represented. Indeed, one might well concede alternativity and still hold that that which is counted, afforded, imputed, or represented is not one or that it has no determinate number independently of a pertinent system. As it stands, alternativity is compatible with singularism, multiplism, or neither. The mere fact that there are differences in the way one conceptualizes does not entail that what is alternatively conceptualized is one common object. The pertinent objects may be common, or uncommon, or it may be undecidable whether they are common or not. In sum, alternativity is compatible with singularism (pluralism) or multiplism, or, in turn, with the undecidability of either of these.

LIMITS OF RIGHTNESS

The title of this book, *Limits of Rightness*, signals that sometimes neither the ideals of singularism nor multiplism apply. They do not apply where the grounds are unavailable to determine whether otherwise competing interpretations actually address a *common* object. If the object is not common or if there are no grounds to determine whether interpretations address a common object, no contest can arise.

"INTERPRETATION"

Finally, a note about "interpretation." It is common to speak of interpretations of different sorts of things, such as poems, works of art, works of music, history, the self, physical particles, numbers, even of "the nature of things" in general. This is in keeping with various definitions of the noun "interpretation" and the verb "to interpret." The *Oxford English Dictionary* defines interpretation in terms of "explanation" and "exposition." It does so further in terms of "construction put upon" that which is interpreted. It does so as well in terms of "representation." The *Oxford English Dictionary* also defines the verb "interpret" in terms of such prepositional phrases as "to expound," "to render clear or explicit," "to elucidate," "to explain," "to bring out the meaning of," "to render," "to obtain significant information from," "to give particular explanation of," "to take in a specific manner," "to construe," and "to signify."

We should note that "interpretation" is contestable. No clear, univocal, and general rules for its correct application are at hand. Yet we may make some headway in the understanding of the range of ideally admissible interpretations by turning our attention (in chapter 3) to "that which is interpreted." But first, to ramify multiplism, let us consider one of its chief proponents and some representative examples.

NOTES

1. Alexander Nehamas, in a presentation on Michael Krausz, *Rightness and Reasons: Interpretation in Cultural Practices,* held at the University of Pennsylvania, February 3, 1995.

2. Bimal Matilal, "Ethical Relativism and Confrontation of Cultures," in ed. Michael Krausz, *Relativism: Interpretation and Confrontation* (Notre Dame: Notre Dame University Press, 1989), 351.

3. Alexander Nehamas, "The Postulated Author: Critical Monism as a Regulative Ideal," *Critical Inquiry,* 8 (autumn 1981), 133–49.

4. Further on this point, see Krausz, *Rightness and Reasons,* 28–29.

5. Nehamas, "The Postulated Author: Critical Monism as a Regulative Ideal," 144.

6. I am indebted to Robert Nozick for this suggestion.

7. David Norton, *Imagination, Understanding, and the Virtue of Liberality* (Lanham, Md.: Rowman & Littlefield, 1996), 84–85.

8. Norton, *Imagination, Understanding, and the Virtue of Liberality*, 98.

9. Norton, *Imagination, Understanding, and the Virtue of Liberality,* 90.

10. Jitendra N. Mohanty, "Levels of Understanding 'Intentionality,'" *The Monist,* 69 (October 1986), 515. Emphasis added. Note that the *Oxford English Dictionary* defines "confer" in terms of "contribute."

Chapter Two

A Multiplist and an Example: Margolis and the Kiefer Paintings

NONCONVERGENCE OF INTERPRETATIONS

Considering cultural objects such as poems, works of visual art, works of music, and the like, Margolis does not require full convergence between competing interpretations. His view contrasts with those of Monroe Beardsley, E. D. Hirsch, and others who agree that ideally there should be full convergence with no logical tension between interpretations. Of them, Margolis says that they have favored

> exclusively correct and comprehensive interpretations; but none has shown why non-converging interpretations cannot be legitimately defended.[1]

Margolis capitalizes on the possibility that nonconverging interpretations can be legitimately defended, not as an interim or tolerable condition approaching an ideal condition of full convergence, but rather as a condition that is itself ideally admissible. Margolis ties this multiplist view to the thought that one cannot clearly individuate a given cultural object; one cannot clearly say what is *in* a given work and what is not. Correspondingly, Margolis holds that cultural objects are both *indeterminate* and *determinable*. Margolis says that

> nothing could be referentially fixed that did not exhibit a certain stability of nature; but *how* alterable (or by what means altered) the life of a person or the restored *Last Supper* or the oft-interpreted *Hamlet* or the theoretically intriguing *Fountain* or the marvelously elastic *Sarrasine* may be is *not* a matter that can be decided, or that is actually determined merely, by fixing such texts or artworks as the reidentifiable referents they are.[2]

Consequently, Margolis urges that one should be as inclusive as possible about ideally admissible interpretations of cultural objects. While he does not countenance contradictory pairs of interpretations (in a bipolar logic), he holds that characteristically bipolar values are inappropriately applied to interpretations of cultural objects. Rather, he invokes values other than truth and its negation (again, understood in a bipolar way) including plausibility, aptness, reasonableness, appropriateness, and their negations. These values are not to be understood as stand-ins for bipolar truth or falsity. And there is no reductive strategy in virtue of which such "plausibility-type" values are reducible to bipolar truth or falsity. With this caveat, Margolis tolerates competition between so-called incongruent interpretations. Margolis tells us that interpretations are incongruent if, on a bipolar logic, they would be contradictory; but on a many-valued logic they are not. Accordingly, Margolis favors the admission of incongruent interpretations. He says:

> Thus, musical interpretations A and B of Brahms's *Fourth Symphony* or literary interpretations A and B of *Hamlet* are incompatible in the straightforward sense that there is no interpretation C in which A and B can be combined. But that is not to say that A and B cannot both be plausible. (The equivocation on "A" and "B" is benign enough.) When, therefore, I say that "we allow seemingly incompatible accounts of a given work . . . to stand as confirmed," I mean to draw attention . . . to the fact that the accounts in question would be incompatible construed in terms of a model of truth and falsity, but are not incompatible construed in terms of plausibility.[3]

IMPUTATION AND THE QUESTION OF PLURALISM

Margolis's thesis of the determinability of cultural objects finds its expression in the thought that aesthetic designs can be *imputed* to particular works. He says:

> There is no reason why, granting that criticism proceeds in an orderly way, practices cannot be sustained in which aesthetic designs are rigorously *imputed* to particular works when they cannot be determinately *found* in them. Also, if they may be imputed rather than found, there is no reason why incompatible designs cannot be jointly defended.[4]

Notice that Margolis speaks of practices in which designs can be imputed. So understood, imputation should be taken as practice-specific rather than person-specific.

One might read the above passage as suggesting that by imputation aesthetic designs become part of the work, and as a consequence it is not the same work. Yet Margolis holds that the work remains the same. And he requires that the resultant object should remain the same even if imputed designs can be incompatible but not contradictory and jointly defended.

But if different features may be imputed to particular works, one wonders if the same or different works obtain. If they are different, then any competition between two interpretations would dissipate. Only an innocuous pluralism would obtain. Different interpretations would be addressing different objects of interpretation. But Margolis affirms that under different imputing interpretations one and the same object may endure. And this is allowed by the introduction of a soft notion of identity, which he calls "unicity." The "same" work may be imputed differently in different circumstances and remain the same in a loose sense, rather in the spirit of Wittgenstein's family resemblance. (See chapter 10.)

Consider two representative cases that Margolis cites, Paul Klee's drawings and Anselm Kiefer's German paintings. (I shall expand upon the latter.) Margolis says :

> I take the Klees to convey not so much a dearth of evidence that I might otherwise have collected as a sense that I am at the limit of what could possibly be added in the way of evidence that could ever bring my interpretive conjectures to any single, final, exclusive truth about these pieces. I am myself impressed with the uncertainty (that is, the certainty) that what Klee produced might not be able to support any uniquely valid description or interpretation or explanation of their "meaning," and that what holds for the Klees holds everywhere for the most part or often enough that we must make conceptual room for such occasions.[5]

For such cases as the Klees, according to Margolis, no one single, final, exclusive truth obtains, not for want of enough evidence. All the evidence that would reasonably count is already in. Rather, the works "might not be able to support any uniquely valid description or interpretation." Notice that this remark of nonsupportability is consistent *both* with the view that the works answer to *more than one* admissible interpretation, as well as with the view that one just *cannot say* if there is one or more admissible interpretations. Put otherwise, the nonsupportability which Margolis mentions does not entail that more than one interpretation is ideally admissible. As well, the question of identity lurks. That is, allowing that aesthetic designs may be imputed, is it one and the same drawing that is taken not to support any uniquely valid interpretation? I shall comment on this question presently. (See also chapter 10.)

THE PAINTINGS OF ANSELM KIEFER

Now consider a second example that Margolis thinks answers to incongruent interpretations. They are the paintings of Anselm Kiefer. Margolis says:

> Imagine someone asks you for the meaning of Anselm Kiefer's use of Nazi symbolism in his enormously intriguing paintings—which may be judged (by opposing lines of reasoning) to be celebrating or exorcising the world's unresolved memories of that terrible past. How should we decide such a dispute?[6]

Lisa Saltzman provides an insightful elaboration of the Kiefer paintings and the historical context of their production and reception.[7] In a summary statement she says:

> Kiefer's work emerged at a moment in postwar German history when conflicting impulses regarding the past and its place in the present were shaping its cultural, social and political landscape. Kiefer's reception then should be seen as at once embedded in and reflective of this context. . . . First, there was a general fear and vigilance about signs of re-nascent or lingering Nazism. Germany, ever wary of its image in an international arena, was quick to condemn any hints of a "return of the repressed." Much like the rioting neo-Nazis whose actions continue to plague Germany, or, perhaps more appropriately, the left-wing anarchists and their misperceived actions, that Kiefer's darkly atavistic work, filled with referents Germanic, could raise the spectre of fascism and the Third Reich, that it could raise truths about certain legacies of a none-too-distant past, that it could compromise the image that Germany so wanted to maintain of itself as a thoroughly transformed society, committed to its constitutional democracy, was motivation enough for its dismissal. . . . For although on some level, his American acceptance seemed to vindicate Kiefer and his work, somehow granting his ambiguous work a stamp of approval, it also raised the spectre of undue American influence, tinged with anti-semitic allusions to a Jewish cabal of powerful art collectors.[8]

And Saltzman adds:

> That Kiefer's work, within the space of little more than a few years, could inspire charges of his being a neo-fascistic ideologue, and then of his being a pawn of sorts of a presumed Jewish–American culture bloc, demonstrates not only the ambivalence of the image of the Jew in the Federal Republic, but just how active the myths and realities of the past were and still are in the Germany of the present.[9]

Saltzman further avers that the situation is made yet more complex by the ambiguity of the American Jewish collectors' attitude toward their own Jewish identity in relation to postwar Germany. Saltzman reports:

> In 1989, [Petra] Kipphoff once again added her voice to the critical field, asserting a very particular tendency in the collecting of Kiefer's work. She wrote: "That [the works of] Anselm Kiefer are today as desired in Jerusalem as in New York or L.A. and that a good half of them can be found in the possession of Jewish collectors, does not at all reduce their ambivalent thematic but instead confirms their ambiguous fascination."[10]

Kiefer's work and his reception cannot be made intelligible independently of their intentional context, that is, of conflicting impulses about postwar German history, Germany's concern for its self-image in an international arena, the role played by non-German critics and collectors in vindicating Kiefer's art, Germany's lingering anti-Semitism, the ambivalence of the supporting Jews about their own identity, their place in postwar Germany, and so forth.

The exorcist and celebratory interpretations of the Kiefer paintings raise interesting questions. Are there logical constraints to actually conjoining the interpretations offered of Kiefer's paintings? Indeed, do Kiefer's works answer to incongruent interpretations? Are the exorcist and the celebratory interpretations really incongruent? Might they be collected into one self-consistent interpretation? Could Kiefer perhaps have been both exorcising and celebrating the Nazi past? Or should we say that we cannot say if they answer to one or more admissible interpretations? Yet the point of Margolis's introduction of this case is to offer an example where opposing (if not contradictory) interpretations are offered of a common object of interpretation. We should ask, too, whether Kiefer's art works are imputed differently by the respective interpretations but still remain "unicitous." And is it in virtue of their unicity that they may remain common (enough) as between the interpretations, and therefore may answer to a multiplist condition? Or, in contrast to Margolis's suggestion, should one reject the thought that interpretations may alter the properties of objects of interpretation in interesting ways (i.e., more than that they take on the trivial property of having been interpreted in one way or another, for example)? And if multiplism is to obtain shall we allow it to do so on other grounds?

NONCONVERGENCE AND MULTIPLISM

The nonconvergence of admissible interpretations is a defining condition of multiplism. But what, exactly, is nonconvergence? And what would be the difference, for example, between the singularist who collects both the exorcist and the celebratory interpretations of Kiefer's paintings, and the multiplist who on account of logical strain between interpretations disallows their aggregation?

As I have said, Margolis unpacks the notion of incongruence in terms of a hypothetical and negative characterization, namely, that, if the designated interpretations were nested in a bivalent logic they would be contradictory, but in a multivalent logic they are not. But we are not told directly what, in a multivalent logic, incongruence comes to. If there is no adequate account of incongruence, the multiplist's effort to keep otherwise contesting interpretations "at odds" with each other could collapse into a singularist condition. So what more can be said, on our part, by way of characterization of incongruence?

Let us look to the intuition that motivates the temptation to formulate the idea of incongruence. Keeping in mind the Kiefer case, one might say that there is a conceptual strain between the exorcist and celebratory interpretations. They are not contradictory in a bivalent sense, for no law of logic is violated by their conjunction. Yet there is a strain between them. What sort of strain is it? It is not merely a psychological strain in the trivial sense that it might be difficult to hold these two interpretations in one's mind at a given time. It is more than that. We may venture a characterization that does not deploy Margolis's hypothetical-and-negative characterization. Namely, two interpretations are incongruent if they are opposed but not exclusive. They could not be exclusive because otherwise only one (if any) interpretation could be admissible. So two interpretations may be opposed yet jointly not violate the law of noncontradiction.

It is ironic that, in one sense, the multiplist must be stricter than the singularist about what should be logically tolerated within a given interpretation. That is, the multiplist should say that, in order to pronounce that these *two* interpretations are admissible, the exorcist interpretation should count as one interpretation, and the celebratory interpretation should count as another interpretation and that they should not be combined as one. In contrast the singularist might be more lax than the multiplist about demands of logical strain within a given interpretation so as to allow that the interpretations might be aggregated into one. So seen, the multiplist should demand stricter requirements about what any comprehensive interpretation should logically tolerate.

The possibility that the singularist might allow incongruent interpretations in his or her comprehensive interpretation takes a good deal of wind out of the multiplist's sail, for then there would be no need for the multiplist to defend the claim that more than one nonconvergent interpretation should be admissible. There would be no need to cast such nonconvergent interpretations in multiplist terms.

Now let us turn to that which is interpreted.

NOTES

1. Joseph Margolis, "Robust Relativism," in *Art and Philosophy: Conceptual Issues in Aesthetics* (Atlantic Highlands, N.J.: Humanities Press, 1980), 157.

2. Joseph Margolis, "Reinterpreting Interpretation," *Journal of Aesthetics and Art Criticism,* 47 (summer 1989), 241–42.

3. Margolis, "Robust Relativism," 164.

4. Margolis, "Robust Relativism," 160. Emphasis added.

5. Joseph Margolis, "Relativism and Cultural Relativity," *JTLA, Journal of the Faculty of Letters, University of Tokyo, Aesthetics*, 22, 1997, 1.

6. Margolis, "Relativism and Cultural Relativity," 16.

7. Lisa Saltzman, *Anselm Kiefer and Art after Auschwitz* (Cambridge: Cambridge University Press, 1999).

8. Saltzman, *Anselm Kiefer and Art after Auschwitz,* 122–23.

9. Saltzman, *Anselm Kiefer and Art after Auschwitz,* 122.

10. Saltzman, *Anselm Kiefer and Art after Auschwitz,* 120.

Chapter Three

That Which Is Interpreted

In order for interpretations to compete, the object to which the interpretations address themselves must be common between them. But the condition of commonality may not be easily satisfied, especially when the objects are determinable or when certain properties may be imputed to them. Paul Thom, for example, embraces a kind of imputationist view of interpretation. It is instructive to see what consequences such a view has with regard to the identity or commonality of the object of interpretation.

Thom introduces a three-tier structure that seeks to articulate the relation between (a) an interpretation, (b) an object-as-represented, and what Thom calls (c) a further object.[1] The further object plays a critical role in his view of reference and predication. Thom assumes that the further object precedes interpretive activity. (This qualifies Thom's view as external constructive realist, as I shall use the phrase as set out in chapter 5.) Further, Thom holds that it is an object-as-represented that may be differently imputed. And while the object-as-represented is not one and the same thing when differently imputed, in an indirect way the interpretations in question still address the same thing, namely the further object that affords and is represented by the objects-as-represented.

Here is a point of terminology. Thom's use of the phrase "further object" roughly corresponds with the phrase "object as such" in my characterization of realism in chapter 4. And his use of the phrase "object-as-represented" roughly corresponds with my use of "intentional objects." Correspondingly, Thom says:

> The important point is that interpretation displays a three-tier structure. For present purposes I am calling the three levels 'interpretation,' 'object-as-represented' and 'further object.' The labels are not vital; the number of levels is.[2]

Thom applies his scheme to the well-known face–vase configuration. He says:

> in discussing a line-drawing which can be seen either as two facing heads or as a vase, Krausz states "the object-of-interpretation is understood in terms of its imputed properties." . . . Now it is true that different aspects of the drawing become salient in the two interpretations, and that if there are different saliences there are different intentional objects. Further it is true that "the interpretation — face or vase — prompts one to impute salience to certain features of the presented configuration, which in turn confirms the propriety of interpreting the configuration as a face or a vase." But if we take this to mean that there are two objects-of-interpretation, then we need to remember that behind these distinct objects-of-interpretation there is a single further object. This, we might say (following Margolis), has been identified in the two interpretations. Further, we could say that the two interpretations represent the further object differently, provided that our concept of representation did not rule out selectivity. The imputed properties (leading to the interpretation "face" or "vase") are, we can agree, part of the object-of-interpretation; but they are no part of this single further object of both interpretations, namely the configuration of lines in the figure. (The same points can be made with reference to Krausz's other examples — Van Gogh's *The Potato Eaters,* Wordsworth's Lucy poems, self-interpretation, and interpretation of other cultures.)[3]

According to Thom, different interpretations impute different aspects of the configuration as salient. If there are different saliences there are different objects-as-represented. The interpretation prompts one to impute salience to certain features of the presented configuration, which in turn confirms the propriety of interpreting the configuration as it is. Different imputations result in different objects-as-represented. Yet behind these distinct objects-as-represented, there is a further object, the configuration. And that has been identified in the two interpretations. The imputed properties are part of the object-as-represented, but they are no part of this further object. In this way Thom offers a reconstruction of the face–vase configuration (and other examples as well) in terms of the distinction between a further object and an object-as-represented.

Yet one might hold that, rather than saying that there is a distinction between the further object and the object-as-represented, what is really going on is that one simply "sees" the properties of the further object. That is, there is no constructed object-as-represented. There is only the object seen one way or another. Put otherwise, the objection might go, there is no need to introduce a separate thing — an object-as-represented — to account for the fact that people see the pertinent configuration differently.

But the point of Thom's introducing the object-as-represented is to capture the thought that certain properties are ascribable to something other than the further object when one assigns salience or significance to a received object. That is, certain properties of the further object may be singled out as salient in relation to certain interpretive concerns. And such properties are not predicated of the further object as such. They are predicated of objects-as-represented. To say that it is interesting or useful to see such and such a further object as an x or as a y is different from saying that the further object as such has the mentioned property. That is, there is nothing in the further object as such that recommends that it should be seen this or that way. Thom goes on to say that

> Krausz himself recognizes that what he calls the object-of-interpretation (what I call the object-as-represented) is 'not spun out of nothing' but rather, 'imputational interpretation involves selecting features of the presented materials with which to fashion an object-of-interpretation.' . . . These 'presented materials' are what I have been calling the further object of interpretation.[4]

It is the properties of the object-as-represented and not those of the further object that are imputed by interpretation. In the present case, the configuration is the further object, which is seen as a pair of faces or as a vase. These are the objects-as-represented. And it is in light of the pertinent interpretations that saliences are imputed and warrant the objects-as-represented in the way they are. In this sense there is a symbiotic relation between objects-as-represented and interpretations.

But Robert Stecker raises the vexing question of how interpretation could change an object's nature or number. More fully, Stecker says:

> The problem is to understand how making a claim about an *object,* even an object-of-interpretation, can give it a property claimed for it. . . . If the claim is true, the object *already* has the property. If it is false, the object does not have the property. If it is neither true nor false, then what difference can be made by saying the object has the property or even telling a plausible story according to which the object has the property? Before an interpretation is offered, an object may well be indeterminate with respect to a property, but if it is, then such saying or story telling will not make *it* determinate, though it may get people to think of the object as determinate.[5]

It appears that Stecker collapses the object-as-represented into the further object and thus generates a paradox from the mistaken thought that it is the properties of the further object that are taken to be imputed. Accordingly, this is how Thom answers Stecker.

> Stecker poses the question of how interpretation can involve both construction and predication—how an interpretation can complete an object-of-interpretation by making a claim about it. As Stecker puts it. . . , 'The problem is to understand how making a claim about an object, even an object-of-interpretation, can give it a property claimed for it.' Our three-tier structure for interpretation provides one answer to this puzzle: the interpretation makes a claim not about the further object but about the object-as-represented, while the latter may go beyond the former.

Interpretation does indeed involve both construction and predication, but at different levels: the object-as-represented is a construction from the further object.

In each case, by processes of selection, suppression, highlighting and contextualization a representation of the painting is constructed, and this representation is then claimed to fall under a specific interpreting concept. This way of thinking   allows interpretation to have both constructive and predicative elements, and thus perhaps provides a solution to Stecker's puzzle. At the same time, it allows for a type of constructive interpretation not mentioned by Stecker—namely where the concept, applied by the interpreter to the object-as-represented, has itself been constructed precisely for this purpose.[6]

Thom clarifies his point when he says:

a predicative relation holds *in the first instance* between the interpretation and the object-as-represented, but . . . it transfers to the further object to the extent that that object is appropriately represented by the object-as-represented. If the representation is appropriate to the type of interpretation being attempted, then the transfer works, otherwise not.[7]

Thom's thought is that the further object indirectly answers to the interpretations in virtue of the fact that the further object is the material out of which the object-as-represented is constructed. Accordingly, as Thom sees it, where multiplism obtains, it does so indirectly between the interpretations of the further object via the object-as-represented. Multiplism does not obtain directly between the interpretations and the object-as-represented. Where objects-as-represented are imputed, different objects-as-represented obtain. That is, pluralism rather than multiplism obtains between interpretation and object-as-represented.

I shall suggest that even if Thom can successfully defend his claim that reference might obtain, even if indirectly, between interpretation and a further object then still neither singularism nor multiplism can apply—if, that is, the further object is not individuable. Without individuation of the supposedly common further object, interpretations could not compete.

By way of anticipation of our further treatment of Margolis, it is worth noting that Thom's idiom of "object-as-represented" resembles Margolis's idiom of "intentional denotatum" as expressed, for example, in Margolis's response to Stecker. Margolis says:

interpretation imputes a determinate sense to what (interpretively) is constituted as an Intentional *denotatum*—determinate as a *denotatum* and, as such, determinable in nature. The distinction is critical and is ignored by those (Stecker, for one) who neglect the complexity of Intentionality or who see no fundamental difference between Intentional and non-Intentional properties. But, of course, that is precisely what is at issue.[8]

Thom summarizes his thesis in the penultimate page of his book, *Making Sense*. Note that Thom uses the term "pluralism" for my term "multiplism" when he says:

> Our three-tier structure—object, object-as-represented, and interpretation—allows us simultaneously to maintain the Principle of Pluralism and that of the Hermeneutic Circle, given a modified version of the Hermeneutic Circle which states that if the interpretation is different then the object-*as-represented* is different. One and the same object can have several interpretations, even if one and the same object-as-represented can't, provided that one and the same object can be represented in several ways. So Pluralism is compatible with the modified Hermeneutic Circle. To this extent, the three-tier structure provides us with a way of preserving both our principles.
>
> By contrast, if we stick to a two-tier structure consisting just of the object and its interpretation then we couldn't maintain *both* the Hermeneutic Circle and Pluralism. We can't maintain Pluralism along with DIDO [Different Interpretation Different Object], since DIDO tells us that if there are several interpretations then there are several objects.[9]

As already remarked, according to Thom, an interpretation and an object-as-represented are symbiotically related. That which is represented as salient is a function of the favored interpretation, and the favored interpretation is affirmed by the object-as-represented, constructed in light of the favored interpretation. For example, in the case of the face–vase configuration, the object-as-represented is the configuration seen as a face or a vase. And it is seen as one or the other in light of a face-interpretation or a vase-interpretation. An interpretation may impute certain properties to an object-as-represented and thereby change the properties of the object-as-represented. This leaves open the nature of the further object. At the same time, the interpretation of one object-as-represented may be jointly defended with another interpretation of another object-as-represented. Under these conditions no direct conflict between interpretations would obtain because the interpretations would not be addressing the same object-as-represented. Yet indirectly interpretations might conflict in virtue of the objects-as-represented having been afforded by a common further object.

In passing we may note that one advantage of adopting Thom's three-tiered scheme is that it allows us to make sense of John Dewey's otherwise troubling view of artworks. Dewey's motivating concern is to enhance human experience, specifically of art products as "finally experienced." He says:

> there is a difference between the art product (statue, painting or whatever) [parallel: "further object"], and the *work* of art [parallel: "object-as-represented"]. The first is physical and potential; the latter is active and experienced. It is what the product does, its working. For nothing enters experience bald and unaccompanied, whether it be a seemingly formless happening, a theme intellectually

systematized, or an object elaborated with every loving care of united thought and emotion. Its very entrance is the beginning of a complex interaction; upon the nature of this interaction depends the character of the thing as finally experienced. When the structure of the object is such that its force interacts happily (but not easily) with the energies that issue from the experience itself; when their mutual affinities and antagonisms work together to bring about a substance that develops cumulatively and surely (but not too steadily) toward a fulfillment of impulsions and tensions, then indeed there is a work of art.[10]

Dewey defines a work of art as a complex, cocreated by the experiencing viewer and the art product. Thus arises a paradox, namely, that on different occasions of experiences of the art product, different artworks obtain. How then can any commonality between artworks be grounded, without which no different interpretations of them could compete? Following Thom, Dewey might say that it can be grounded by the common art product (further object, say) that affords the artworks in different experiential contexts.

Thom wishes to preserve both a modified hermeneutic circle and the principle of pluralism (again, "multiplism" in my use). Since, on his account, the hermeneutic circle entails that different interpretations mandate different objects-as-represented, multiplism with respect to objects-as-represented cannot be sustained. Multiplism requires that that which is variously interpreted be about the same thing. Yet Thom does *indirectly* ground multiplism, that is, in the sameness of that which is *indirectly* interpreted, namely in the further object.

The question arises how Thom can establish that the further object is singular or, for that matter, even countable. The sameness of that which is indirectly interpreted may not be grounded or known to be grounded in a single further object. The further object must be singular if it is to perform the job of "grounding" the objects-as-represented. If the further object is not singular, then Thom's pluralism (again, my multiplism) could not be generated. But Thom provides no grounds for individuating further objects. He simply assumes that it is one and only one further object that affords and is represented by objects-as-represented. If one successfully argued either that more than one further object were in place, or that there were no way of counting the further object, then the job that Thom assigns to the further object could not be performed. Put otherwise, Thom's principle of pluralism (or my multiplism) cannot be sustained if one were to disallow the countability and singularity of the further object.

I follow Thom in distinguishing between a further object and an object-as-represented. But Thom fails to effect a multiplism between interpretations and further objects, precisely because further objects do not come with the requisite individuation necessary for multiplism. That is, further objects are not given with identity conditions such that, of two competing interpretations one cannot say that they are addressing the same thing.

I characterize Thom's view as constructive realist, which (as I shall develop it in chapters 4–9) holds that the very idea of *objects* of interpretation or the *existence* of such objects makes no sense independently of some constructing framework or symbol system. There are intramural differences between constructive realists. The *internal* constructive realist holds that it makes no sense to posit that there is *anything* beyond constructing interpretive frameworks. In contrast, the *external* constructive realist holds that one must posit that there is something beyond constructing frameworks (Putnam calls them "inputs"), but he or she withholds predicates of *objecthood* or *existence* for these are taken by constructive realists generally to be internal to constructing frameworks. The thought is not that to qualify as an external constructive realist one must assume that there are *objects* that precede interpretive activity, or that they exist. Again, objecthood and existence would be countenanced by constructive realists, whether internal or external, only within symbol systems. Rather, it would be enough to concede that, as I say, there is some presystematic material to be appealed to in order to account for the construction of the real. It would not be required that one should posit some "most basic objects" since objecthood itself would be parasitic of symbol systems. Yet Thom resists my characterizing his view as external constructive realist on the grounds that

> An external object of interpretation in my sense does not have to be independent of all representation. My distinction between external objects and objects-as-represented carries no implications about whether there is or could be an object that is independent of all representations.[11]

Quite so. But the point is not so much whether there is or could be an *object* that is independent of all representations. Rather, it is whether there is anything there at all that in interpretive contexts could be constructed into an object. The requirement for external constructive realism is more minimal than Thom makes out. He does say, "I could . . . believe that objects-of-interpretation are always or sometimes themselves representations of something prior."[12] It is unclear what Thom packs into his last phrase, "something prior." If he means that for any object-as-represented there is nothing to be bestowed as an object or as an individuated existent, then Thom's constructive realism would be internal. On the other hand if he means that for some objects-as-represented there is something (not yet bestowed as an object or an individuated existent) then his constructive realism would be external. That would be enough. Another way to put the point is to ask Thom whether, when he denies that he is a realist, he understands realism to be the thesis that there are *objects* whose *existence* is independent of interpretive practices or whether there is anything there independent of interpretive practices—without packing into the "thereness" any presumption of objecthood or individuated existence. However that clarification comes out, though, I expect that Thom would agree that in order for singularism or multiplism to apply as interpretive ideals, interpretanda (internal or external) need to be individuated. To anticipate, the more general point that I shall develop in chapters 4–9 is that neither singularism nor multiplism entails either realist, constructivist, or constructive–realist types of ontologies. And, unless further freighted, none of these types of ontologies entail either singularism or multiplism.

THE QUESTION OF ONTOLOGY

It is now time to consider the ontological grounding of the "further object" (or its analogs) in various ontological treatments. Accordingly, the following chapters will take up the question of the relation between interpretive ideals and realism, constructivism, and versions of constructive realism. One might ask why one should take up this question at all if (a) one accepts the distinction between objects-as-represented and further objects, and if (b) one affirms that it is objects- as-represented that interpretations are about in the first instance. Granting (a) and (b) there would be no need to pursue the question of the relation between interpretive ideals and the ontology of further objects. But these conditions are contentious. And their acceptance or rejection depends upon the ontologies in question. Yet despite differences over (a) and (b), we will find that the ontologies are detachable from singularism and multiplism.

NOTES

1. I take it that Thom's choice of word, in "further *object*," is innocent. It might have been better if Thom had spoken of a more neutral "materia," as I shall say, which would be understood more as a place holder without connotation of individuable *objects*.

2. Paul Thom, "Review of Michael Krausz," in *Rightness and Reasons: Interpretation in Cultural Practices* (Ithaca: Cornell University Press, 1993); Joseph Margolis, *Interpretation Radical But Not Unruly* (Berkeley: University of California Press, 1994); and Robert Stecker, "The Constructivist's Dilemma," *Literature and Aesthetics, The Journal of the Sydney Society of Literature and Aesthetics* (October 1997), 183.

3. Thom, "Review," 182–83.

4. Thom, "Review," 183.

5. Robert Stecker, "The Constructivist's Dilemma," *Journal of Aesthetics and Art Criticism,* 55/1 (winter 1997), 50. Emphasis added.

6. Thom, "Review," 184–85.

7. Paul Thom, personal communication, October 20, 1998.

8. Joseph Margolis, *What, After All, Is a Work of Art?* (University Park: Pennsylvania State University Press, 1999), 100.

9. Paul Thom, *Making Sense: A Theory of Interpretation* (Lanham, Md.: Rowman & Littlefield, 2000), 107.

10. John Dewey, *Art as Experience* (New York: Capricorn Books, 1934), 162.

11. Paul Thom, "Rightness and Success in Interpretation," in ed. Michael Krausz, *Is There a Single Right Interpretation?* (University Park: Pennsylvania State University Press, 2001), ms. 12.

12. Thom, "Rightness and Success in Interpretation," ms. 12.

Chapter Four

Realism and Constructivism

I have suggested that the characteristic or orthodox associations of singularism with realism and multiplism with constructivism are not necessary. One could coherently adopt one of four combinations: singularism–realism, multiplism–realism, singularism–constructivism, and multiplism–constructivism. Thus, it appears that we may detach the question of interpretive ideals from the dispute between realists and constructivists. In the next six chapters I shall consider the possibility that the ontological field might not be exhaustively comprised by realism and constructivism. That is, I shall consider versions of an irenic ontology—constructive realism—and ask of them whether they entail either singularism or multiplism. If they entail neither, then the issue of ideality remains detachable from ontology. Also, throughout these discussions we should be mindful of the commonality of that which is interpreted (as problematized in our discussion of Thom), without which different interpretations could compete.

To help articulate realism and constructivism, consider an intriguing example. In December 1996 I visited Benares, India, the holy city of the Hindus. With two friends I took an early morning boat ride up the Ganges River to inspect the ghats, the stations along the river at which worshippers and bathers congregate. The ghats include connecting stone steps, sometimes quite grand. Several of these ghats are famous for the funeral pyres at which the dead are cremated. As one body is being consumed by fire, the next body awaits its turn. We urged our boatman to navigate the boat close to Manikarnika Ghat, one of the more famous and busier ghats. As our boat neared the first step my friend whispered in dismay that I should look over the side. There, between other parked boats in muddied waters with decaying vegetation and debris, was a dead baby with bits of wrapping attached to it. The baby appeared to be just a few weeks old. It was quite stiff. That is what I saw. I was shocked.

In the days that followed I asked several Indian people to make sense of what I had seen. First, I was told that while this is not a common sight it is not rare. Indeed, it follows a practice. According to Hindu tradition in which local Buddhists also participate, the Ganges River is the embodiment of life force itself. It is the source from which life begins, and it is the vehicle that transports the soul from one embodiment to another. The river is, in short, a hallowed medium for transmigration. More than that: it is thought that dying and being cremated in Banares will guarantee release from the cycle of birth and death. For this reason the sick and elderly make pilgrimages to die in Banares, where their passage to the next embodiment will be properly ensured. Further, cremation is thought of as a process of moral purification. Since babies are not morally contaminated to begin with, they are in no need of the purification of cremation. Indeed, as morally pure beings they may be accorded the *honor* of being returned directly to the life source of the Ganges. The same honor is bestowed upon such holy people as Hindu Saddhus and Buddhist monks. The bodies of these honored beings are completely wrapped in appropriate cloth, tied tightly, and weighed down by heavy stones. Sometimes, as in the present case, the wrapping comes undone and the body floats to the surface.

Now what did I actually see? Did I, the initially untutored North American, see something different from what the Indian saw? Or did we see the same thing but interpret it differently? If we saw the same thing but interpreted it differently, who is right? Or is more than one interpretation admissible?

These questions became yet more sharply focused for me when, some months later, a parallel case was reported in the *Philadelphia Daily News,* Monday, March 31, 1997, the day after Easter Sunday. The headline read, "Newborn Found Dead in Cobbs Creek." The reporter wrote, "One newborn spent Easter Sunday naked and silent, his lifeless body floating in the muddy, shallow waters of Cobbs Creek in Philadelphia's Eastwick section." After giving an account of the discovery of the baby, the article continued,

> Police said they could not immediately determine whether the baby had been thrown into the creek alive or whether he had been born dead and then dumped. There were no obvious signs of injury. "It's obvious the baby was dumped in the creek, but as to whether this was immediately after it was born, I don't know," said Police Lt. Paul Domenic. . . . Anyone who might have information about who dumped the newborn may call homicide detectives.[1]

No such concept as "dumped" is appropriate in the Ganges River case. Indeed, in the Ganges River case one might say the newborn was "honored" by being returned to a hallowed place. When asking for useful leads for homicide detectives, the Philadelphia article implicates investigative, legal, and possibly penal institutions. No such implications are suggested in the religious context of the Ganges River case.

In treating such cases let us be mindful of the danger of sanitizing or homogenizing a culture or its individual members. The "point of view" or the "conceptual scheme" or the "symbol system" of the Indian and the North American is, to start with, an abstraction. And even at that it is not impermeable or homogeneous. When confronted with the Ganges River case some Indians may be shocked and some not. Some North Americans may be shocked and some not. Further an Indian or a North American may regard the baby as both (incongruently) honored and dumped, simultaneously or serially, perhaps reaching for an irenic accommodation of the two possibilities, or perhaps not. Further, the heterogeneity of individual viewpoints might well cloud one's ability to clearly distinguish corresponding objects of interpretation. But for present purposes of articulating the dialectic between realism and constructivism, let us set aside the issue of the homogeneity or the heterogeneity of viewpoints. It will not bear on the articulation of realism or constructivism.

AN INITIAL CONTRAST BETWEEN
REALISM AND CONSTRUCTIVISM

How, then, should this intriguing comparative example be understood? Two approaches suggest themselves. The first approach is realist. In brief, it may be understood in terms of a distinction between an *object as such* (recall Thom's allied notion of "further object") and an *object as represented*. An object as such would be an object independent of any representation of it. In the present case the realist would say that there is an object as such, a baby, and it may be represented in different ways depending upon different cultural circumstances. The second approach is constructivist. In brief, it holds that the distinction between an object as such and an object as represented is a distinction without a difference. All would-be objects as such are tantamount to objects as represented. On the constructivist view it would be better to drop all talk of objects as such. If objects as represented are taken to talk about the same or different things, they do so depending upon the agreement or disagreement between objects as represented. Accordingly, the North American and the Indian see the same baby just in case their objects as represented agree, but not in virtue of there being an object as such independently of any representations.

More fully, the realist holds that objects as such are "given." They are uninterpreted "facts of the matter." Their properties—or at least a determining subset of their properties—are autonomous of representation or interpretive practice. On the other hand, objects as represented are "taken" in a certain way within a particular cultural setting. So understood, the baby in the Ganges, the object as such, is taken as or is represented as, an honored being.

The baby in Cobbs Creek, the object as such, is taken as or is represented as "dumped." And in having been taken in significantly different ways the objects as such are refigured into different objects as represented.

While realism affirms that interpreters cannot bestow or impute or confer properties upon objects as such, it allows that they may impute properties to objects as represented depending upon the symbol system in which they are nested. But the realist holds that however one represents the babies in the Ganges River or Cobbs Creek, there is a baby as such in the Ganges and there is a baby as such in Cobbs Creek. The rest is representation or interpretation.

A constructivist might say that, in virtue of a favored Hindu/Buddhist interpretation, the baby in the Ganges is constituted as a Hindu/Buddhist object of interpretation. It is in virtue of such imputation that one might discern it to be the baby that it is. In contrast, a realist might say that the baby is what it is, independently of any Hindu/Buddhist or North American interpretations. The baby has not taken on different properties in virtue of imputation. Rather, followers of the Hindu and Buddhist traditions regard the baby as an honored being. This does not mean that there is a change in the nature of the baby. It means only that the baby, constituted as it is, is regarded in a certain way and accorded a certain place in a favored tradition. It is the representation of the babies and not some change in the nature of the babies that is at issue. It is not the case that imputation mandates a change in the thing interpreted.

The contrast between the realist's and constructivist's approaches can be further seen in the case of paintings. The realist would say that it is best to see interpretations of the *Potato Eaters*, for example, as proposing ways to represent the work rather than ways of constituting the work. In proposing that the work might appropriately be interpreted as a Marxist painting, for example, one is proposing that it would be instructive or useful or interesting to take certain features of the work as salient (the rough hands, for example). But taking certain of the painting's properties as salient is not to change the properties of the painting. It is to designate the object as represented. And that is not constituting the painting as such. However differently interpreters might take the painting, its properties as such are not thereby altered.

Consider yet another example. Realism holds that there were carbon atoms before there were theories about them, that is, before carbon atoms were represented in terms of the periodic table of elements. Whatever symbol systems might be devised for the representation of things, the nature of the things represented does not depend upon their representation. Accordingly, John Searle formulates realism this way. "The world (or alternatively, reality or the universe) exists independently of our representations of it."[2]

Notice that *this* definition of realism—which emphasizes representation-independence—allows that the world (or reality or the universe) or designated portions of it may be *indeterminate* in the sense that it lacks clear boundary conditions. (See chapter 10.) Indeed, the idea that a representation or an interpretation must be *about* the world or some designated portion of it does not entail that the world must be fully determinate.

Perhaps unwittingly Searle seems to foreclose the possibility of linking realism with multiplism when he offers a distinctly different formulation of realism just a few pages later.

> *Realism is the view that there is a way that things are that is logically independent of all human representations. Realism does not say how things are but only that there is a way that they are.*[3]

In speaking of "the way things are" Searle invites speculation that, while realism takes things to be logically independent of all human representation, those things may be either determinate or indeterminate. Now the claim that things are representation-independent is compatible with the claim either that there is *a* single way that things are or with the claim that there is more than one way that things are. Searle himself does not discuss the implications of the differences in his formulations. But they open up a fruitful line of inquiry about the relations between realism, indeterminacy, and multiplism. (See chapter 10.) Namely, realism is compatible with both indeterminacy and determinacy. It is compatible also with singularism and multiplism. We shall see, however, whether realism is compatible with multiplism in virtue of the indeterminacy of its objects.

For now we may observe that realism is consistent with either determinacy or indeterminacy. If realism were actually conjoined with the claim of indeterminacy, and if such a claim of indeterminacy were taken to entail multiplism (a suggestion that I shall contest), then realism would entail multiplism and not singularism. Yet the claim of indeterminacy is consistent with either multiplism or singularism. And realism is compatible with either singularism or multiplism.

ON COMPARING THE REPRESENTED
WITH THE UNREPRESENTED

Some arguments against realism mistakenly assume that without access to the way the world is (or its objects are), realism cannot be defended. For example, R. G. Collingwood says

> that Cook Wilson's central positive doctrine, "knowing makes no difference to what is known," was meaningless. I [R.G.C.] argued that any one who claimed, as Cook Wilson did, to be sure of this, was in effect claiming to know what he was simultaneously defining as unknown. For if you know that no difference is made to a thing ⊖ by the presence or absence of a certain condition c, you know what ⊖ is like with c, and also what ⊖ is like without c, and on comparing the

two find no difference. This involves knowing what ⊖ is like without c; in the present case, knowing what you defined as the unknown.⁴

But Collingwood's argument does not show what he thinks it does. It does not show the meaninglessness or falsity of realism. It only shows that one cannot know it to be true by the method of comparison between the known and the unknown, or between the represented and the unrepresented. Further, Collingwood's argument cuts both ways. It cuts against constructivism too. For the claim that representing or knowing *does* make a difference to what is represented or known also presumes as well that one can compare the object before and after the condition c. But, for the same reasons that Collingwood adduces, one is never in a position to make such a comparison. Thus, Collingwood's argument against realism, according to the method of comparison, turns out to be an argument not against the meaningfulness or truth of realism but against its knowability, and it holds also against the knowability of constructivism.

REALISM NOT A METHODOLOGY

Notice that realism (and for that matter constructivism as well) is not a methodological procedure. That is, the realist affirms that there must be representation-independent objects without which one could not make sense of the idea of aboutness. It provides an answer to the philosophical rather than the methodological question of what a representation is *about*. At the same time, realism does not help to sort out which *particular* distributive representations should be admitted and which not. That is, the realist could well agree that realism does no *methodological* work. Indeed, realist Popper affirms as much when he says:

> within methodology we do not have to presuppose metaphysical realism; nor can we, I think, derive much help from it, except of an intuitive kind. For once we have been told that the aim of science is to explain, and that the most satisfactory explanation will be the one that is most severely testable and most severely tested, we know all that we need to know as methodologists. That the aim is realizable we cannot assert, neither with nor without the help of metaphysical realism which can give us only some intuitive encouragement, some hope, but no assurance of any kind. And although a rational treatment of methodology may be said to depend upon an assumed, or conjectured, aim of science, it certainly does not depend upon the metaphysical and most likely false assumption that the true structural theory of the world (if any) is discoverable by man, or expressible in human language.⁵

The *methodological* question as to which of competing interpretations one should accept or reject does not hang on one's ontological characterization of the pertinent objects. Indeed, both realist and constructivist historians, for example, work with the same evidence, and it is only that evidence that comes into play when they address the methodological question of adjudicating between competing distributive historical claims. Whether historians are realists or constructivists in philosophical moments does not enter their methodological activity. While the realist may talk about correspondence of interpretation to past actuality, and while the constructivist may talk of fittingness of one interpretation with other warranted beliefs, which of the particular historical claims are embraced depends not upon the ontological characterization offered. In other words, for methodological purposes, all that is needed is a serviceable distinction between sustainable or unsustainable evidence, and that is not uniquely mandated by either realism or constructivism.

Yet the realist insists that his position does the *philosophical* work of accounting for aboutness. On Popper's account any statement that refers must be understood in a realist way. Popper thinks that a claim that is *of* something commits one to realism. He says:

> human language is essentially descriptive (and argumentative), and an unambiguous description is always realistic: it is *of* something—of some state of affairs which may be real or imaginary. Thus, if the state of affairs is imaginary, then the description is simply false and its negation is a true description of reality.[6]

In contrast, the constructivist holds that one may well allow that a claim is about something, but aboutness is not uniquely captured by realism. The constructivist affirms that a serviceable distinction between the real and the imaginary, or between true and false, can be drawn within a constructivist rubric. The constructivist holds that there is no reason to assume that the realist's understanding of the real is uniquely defensible. (See the discussion of "Intentional Layering" later in this chapter.)

The level of discourse at which realism and constructivism are in contest is not the level at which particular distributive claims are made. Proponents of these ontological theories may agree about distributive claims while disagreeing about their ontological construals.

OBJECTS AS SUCH AS PHYSICAL STIMULANTS

A realist might be tempted to distinguish an object as such from an object as represented by suggesting that an object as such is a physical stimulant for the object as represented. A physical stimulant may be taken to be the object as such that, in combination with other conditions, causes different ways of looking at it.

Here the realist faces the constructivist objection that objects as such cannot be fixed independently of their representations. Even concrete middle-sized objects as such do not present themselves independently of some symbol system. The realist might seek to overcome this objection by suggesting that one might indeed identify the object as such by ostention, by pointing. But ostention is not enough. For, as the later Wittgenstein famously showed, one needs a supplementing story to identify which of the possible things pointed to one is being shown. As Wittgenstein says:

> There are, of course, what can be called "characteristic experiences" of pointing to (e.g.) the shape. For example following the outline with one's finger or with one's eyes as one points.—But *this* does not happen in all cases in which I "mean the shape," and no more does any other one characteristic process occur in all these cases.—Besides, even if something of the sort did recur in all cases, it would still depend on the circumstances—that is, on what happened before and after the point-ing—whether we should say "He pointed to the shape and not to the colour."
>   To repeat: in certain cases, especially when one points "to the shape" or "to the number" there are characteristic experiences and ways of pointing—"char-acteristic" because they recur often (not always) when shape or number are "meant." But do you also know of an experience characteristic of pointing to a piece in a game *as a piece in a game?* All the same one can say: "I mean that this piece is called the 'king', not this particular bit of wood I am pointing to."[7]

Ostention alone does not individuate. Were one to point to the baby in the Ganges and say, "That is what I am talking about," such ostention alone would not settle what would be pointed to. The Hindu could say, you are pointing to an honored being. The secular North American could say you are pointing to a dumped infant. Each assumes a different intentional background. Alterna-tively, when one points to a stone gray wall, for example, it is an open ques-tion whether one is pointing to the stones in it, or a particular stone, to the wall's grayness, or the color contrasts between the different gray stones, or the overall design formed by the mortar around the stones, and so on. Only by as-suming a supplementing intentional story to the pointing does one get indi-viduation. Ostention may well circumscribe. But it does not individuate. These sorts of considerations give rise to the constructivist alternative.

THE CONSTRUCTIVIST APPROACH

More fully, then, in contrast to realism, constructivism holds that objects are never "given." They are always "taken" in a certain way, taken in terms of some representation in some symbol system. Constructivism concludes that, in philosophical contexts, one should stop talking of objects as such. There is no point to talking about the baby in the Ganges as an object as such. Even minimally, as a baby, the object is always represented somehow. No object is presented independent of some representation of it. So, it is urged, the dis-tinction between objects as such and objects as represented is a distinction without a difference.

Notice that constructivism does not entail idealism or subjectivism. Idealism is the view that the inherently real is the mental. Subjectivism is the view that the symbol system in which that which is interpreted is nested is itself relativized to a single person. Constructivism entails neither of these. To say that something is constructed is not to say that it is mental or that it is relative to a single person.

FOUND AND MADE

The distinction between found and made may be thought to distinguish realism from constructivism. Yet the constructivist complains that this distinction is flawed, for one cannot in particular cases distinguish the line between the found and the made. One might hold that the "found" part of the distinction is not a genuine alternative to the made, for the found is represented nowhere. That is, nowhere are facts of the matter presented to us. The very activity of re-presentation itself constitutes an instance of intervention. So the cognate distinction, representation/intervention, turns out to be a distinction without a difference. It's intervention (of one sort or another) all the way down.

Constructivist Nelson Goodman, for example, affirms that the idea of an object as such makes no sense. No would-be object as such can be made intelligible independently of some symbol system.[8] The baby in the Ganges or the baby in Cobbs Creek cannot be made intelligible independent of some symbol system. The intelligibility of any putative object as such will depend upon its being nested in some symbol system, which is to say it is no object as such. It's construction all the way down. There is no way of making sense of an uninterpreted "fact of the matter." Might as well let the object as such drop out of the account. Or, as Goodman says, "We do better to focus on versions rather than worlds."[9]

ALTERNATIVITY OF DESCRIPTIONS

Goodman holds that no one representation, or as he calls it "world-version," is the singular right one. One cannot prioritize the physical description of the baby in the Ganges as a bundle of molecules over its intentional description. The point applies to other middle-sized objects as well. Sticks and stones are describable in terms of their molecular structures as defined by the periodic table of elements, including carbon, hydrogen, and so forth. They are also describable as being combustible and hard. But combustibility and hardness are not properties of neutrons, protons, and electrons. Combustibility and hardness are emergent properties of middle-sized objects at another level of description. Combustibility and hardness are not reducible to molecular descriptions. Which of these descriptions is the right one? Which is most basic? Goodman holds that there is no most basic description, for there is no most basic symbol system in which the descriptions are nested.

Notice that Goodman's constructivism is global in that it covers all types of objects. He provides his own collection of intriguing examples. He tells the story of a friend who was caught speeding.

> A friend of mine was stopped by an officer of the law for driving 56 miles an hour. She argued, "But officer, taking the car ahead of me as fixed, I was not moving at all." "Never mind that," replied the officer. "You were going 56 miles an hour along the road, and (as he stamped his foot) this is what is fixed." "Oh, come now, officer; surely you learned in school that this road as part of the earth is not fixed at all but is rotating rapidly eastward on its axis. Since I was driving westward, I was going slower than those cars parked over there." "O.K. lady, I'll give them all tickets for speeding right now—and you get a ticket for parking on the highway."[10]

This example beautifully illustrates Goodman's view that the identities of middle-sized objects are fixed within some symbol system. They do not inhere in any putative object as such. At the same time, one's stance toward a symbol system may vary. Goodman explicates his thought this way:

> Although a stance may be taken anywhere, and shifted often and without notice, it is not arbitrary. Most of our stances and shifts of stance are habitual, instilled in practice. We commonly take the earth as fixed in describing the motion of a plane, but on the airplane we automatically take the plane as fixed in describing the motions of the cabin crew. Where a choice of stance is more deliberate, it may involve complex considerations of simplicity, convenience, suitability to context, efficacy for a purpose, and accessibility by those we must communicate with. Taking the tip of a fly's wing as fixed in describing the motion of bodies in the solar system would presumably fail on all these counts.[11]

Now, Goodman's view may strike one as odd, as counterintuitive, as puzzling. He responds to that puzzlement in this way:

> You are likely not to go along with this but to protest: "How can there be no fact, no content, but only alternative ways of describing nothing? Surely there must be something that is described, however many different ways there are of describing it. There must be some line between what there is and how to describe it."
>
> Quite so. [Two alternative versions] are alternatives in that they describe something in common: that they are about the same object, that they agree with certain observations, measurements, and principles, that they are in some way descriptive of the same facts. Yet these objects, observations, measurements, principles are themselves conventional; these facts are creatures of their descriptions. Two versions are "of the same facts" to the extent that they share some terms, comprise some identical or kindred concepts, can be translated into one another. All convention depends upon fact, yet all fact is convention.[12]

CONSTRUCTIVISM AND ABOUTNESS

The constructivist holds that there is no reason to posit a representation-independent object that versions are about. Representations are about things that in turn are represented. It's representations all the way down. There is no reason to limit aboutness to objects as such (or to what Thom refers to as "further objects").

The constructivist idea of aboutness may be unpacked in terms of what one might call *intentional layering*. For example, the baby in the Ganges is seen by the Hindu as an honored being, and the Ganges itself is seen by the Hindu as a hallowed medium. At the same time, the baby and the river are chemical states, intelligible in virtue of their being nested in the symbol system of the periodic table of elements.

Consequently, an object may be intentionally layered in virtue of its being nested in layered symbol systems. So, for the constructivist, it is not the case that there was *nothing* that had been intentionalized. There was an intentional *something* that was further intentionalized. And that is a something, not a nothing. Generally, then, an intentional object may answer to multiple layers of intentionality. Nowhere does the object as such "begin" independent of some symbol system. Nowhere does the uninterpreted object as such appear in the constructivist account.

This suggestion of intentional layering concedes to the realist that there is a something beneath a particular world-version that it is about, but it is still an intentionalized something. The particular features of that intentionalized something are made so in virtue of its being nested in some symbol system. In any event, symbol systems are inescapably implicated in the character of any considered object.

The realist will object. Although it may well be that descriptions of an object as such will be cast in some symbol system, at the end of the day there must be an asymptote on which various descriptions converge. And that must be a representation-independent object. That is, the realist might posit that, at the limit, when intentionality is fully minimized, there must be an object as such.

But the constructivist will counter in turn that no object as such can be reached. So what is the constructivist to make of the agreement between the Indian and the North American that there is a baby in the Ganges? Is that not an opening for a realist understanding of an object as such? Goodman would say no. All that agreement shows is that there is agreement between the pertinent symbol systems. Agreement of symbol systems may secure grounds for interpersonal or intersystem dialogue, but it does not mandate realism. One should resist the thought that the agreement between symbol systems betrays an approximation to a "most basic" object as such. And, whichever symbol systems one assumes is, as Goodman says, a matter of "simplicity, convenience, suitability to context, efficacy for a purpose, and accessibility by those we must communicate with."[13] Goodman's associate, Catherine Elgin, makes a parallel claim when she says:

> What justifies the categories we construct is the cognitive and practical utility of the truth they enable us to formulate, the elegance and informativeness of the accounts they engender, the value of the ends they promote. We engage in system building, when we find the resources at hand inadequate.[14]

What status should one attach to such metatheoretical values as (for Goodman) simplicity, convenience, suitability to context, efficacy for a purpose, and accessibility by those we must communicate with; or (for Elgin) cognitive and practical utility, elegance and informativeness? Do not these presumed values invite the thought that some overarching symbol system–independent criteria have been introduced? For both Goodman and Elgin the answer is clear. These values arise only from practical considerations in the negotiations of symbol systems. Their endurance is a mark of their practical utility in negotiating conflicts between symbol systems. They recommend themselves only as guides in forthcoming confrontations and reconciliations.

The North American and the Hindu or Buddhist agree that there is a baby in the Ganges. They do describe something in common. But, on Goodman's view, that commonality is not fixed in virtue of there being an inherent and autonomous object as such, independent of any symbol system. On the contrary, they are common in virtue of an agreement or overlap between the pertinent symbol systems as regards certain observations, measurements, and principles. And, as Goodman emphasizes, observations, measurements, and principles are themselves conventional. As he says, again, "Two versions are 'of the same facts' to the extent that they share some terms, comprise some identical or kindred concepts, can be translated into one another."[15]

Notice that on Goodman's view the agreement between symbol systems provides the conceptual space in which particular things may be said to be *real* in contrast with the illusory, but not in contrast with the unconstructed. The real would not be understood to implicate a symbol system–independent order. Accordingly, one should not confuse the assertion that particular things are real with the theory of realism. Contructivism is compatible with the affirmation that particular things are real. Clearly, for the constructivist, claims that particular things are real rather than illusory are not uniquely affirmable by realists.

In short, according to the constructivist, any attempt to drive a conceptual wedge between objects as such and objects as represented will fail, for any described object as such will be a represented object. It is nested in a symbol system of some kind or other. This is inescapable. Nothing intelligible can be said about the world independent of world-versions. We might as well let the idea of an uninterpreted world or objects as such drop out of all accounts. Any attempt to say what a version is a version of will issue in yet another version!

In short, no symbol system, no talk of symbol system–independent objects. About such things it is best to remain silent. It is best to let go of the temptation to speak of them. I call this the *constructivist's reductio* (of realism).

A REALIST RESPONSE TO CONSTRUCTIVISM

The realist might concede that the distinction between an object as such and an object as represented might make no methodological difference in that it could not distinguish a particular admissible from an inadmissible distributive claim. But to concede that much is a far cry from saying that the distinction is a distinction without a difference. That is, the distinction is offered as part of an *account* rather than a *method*. The situation is rather like that found in the theory of truth. That is, one might agree that adopting a correspondence theory of truth over a coherence theory of truth or vice versa, say, will not help to determine which particular distributive claims about the world are in fact true or false (whether, for example, Banares is situated on the shores of the Ganges River). But that is a far cry from saying that, as an *account* of truth, it makes no difference which theory one embraces. Despite the fact that one may or may not have access to objects as such, the realist urges that objects as such are after all what interpretations are *about*. In short, the constructivist's rejection of the realist distinction between objects as such and objects as represented arises from a confusion that fails to distinguish a *philosophical account* from a *methodological procedure*.

Second, the realist might observe that all that the so-called constructivist's reductio shows is that what is *said* is inevitably nested in some symbol system. That does not show that there is nothing that is not nested in some symbol system. The realist might affirm that it is possible that there are objects in the world that nobody has thought of, despite the fact that that assertion is presently made in some symbol system, and despite the fact that it is made by using the concept of "objects." The realist could hold that despite our conceiving of them in the present thought experiment, there are specific rocks in the Himalayan Mountains that may yet come to be discovered. And their being there is a matter quite separate from anyone's conceiving of them or from their representations being nested in some symbol system deploying the concept "rocks." Even if, as Goodman says, there are shared terms or kindred concepts and mutual translatability between representations or world-versions, that is not enough. The rocks (or something, however described) are *there*, just as the Himalayan Mountains (or something, however described) is *there*, independent of any representations of them.

Third, the realist may observe that the idea of agreement between symbol systems, in virtue of which objects as represented may be taken to address a common thing, cannot be sustained. For, as Goodman's own account reflects, symbol systems are not fully translatable. The physical and the phenomenal, for example, designate different types of world-versions. That fact is needed to show that there is no single privileged world-version. But that same fact disallows that there can be full commensuration between world-versions that could fix an object as represented as common. Many world-versions issue in many objects as represented without the possibility of full agreement between any pair of symbol systems. This disallows fixing all objects as represented as common between world-versions.

Fourth, the constructivist claims that the realist's assertion that there is something that precedes representation or is outside of a symbol system *itself* is inevitably symbol system–dependent or representation-dependent. That is, the constructivist claims that the realist is being contradictory in asserting, *from within* a symbol system, that there is a symbol system–independent order of things. Here the realist might respond as follows. The claim that there is a symbol system–independent or representation-independent order of things does not mandate that the claim to that effect cannot itself be symbol system–dependent. And, given this concession, there is no reason why one might not hypothesize that there is an order of things independent of (or preceding) symbol systems or representations. The realist affirms that one can speak of representation independence from inside a symbol of representation.

In this regard a realist might embrace the early Wittgensteinian thought that there are simples in the world that map one–to–one with the units of language to picture the totality of facts in the world. But expressing this is itself beyond the limits of language. Language can only "show" not "say" what these simples are like. So understood, the properties of these simples are independent of interpretive practices, and they are not describable in principle. Seen in this way, realism might be combined with a claim of ineffability.

Fifth, the realist might seek to ground realism by capitalizing on such universals as are exemplified in diverse languages. For example, there are no known languages without some form of an indexical to indicate the agency, the "I" of the speaker; or some cognate form of a subject and a predicate, and so on. Such universals, the realist might urge, could not be sustained unless they reflected some approximate match with a representation-independent order. A realist might concede that such universality does not entail realism. Rather, it only indicates a commonality or convergence. Still, in the absence of a more compelling alternative explanation of such convergence, realism stands as the most plausible explanation.

Sixth, the realist may offer a related argument, namely, realism is vindicated by the success of evolution. That is, our collective survival attests to the truth of realism. Again, the realist may concede that while successful evolution is compatible with realism, it does not entail realism. Given such a concession, the realist may still affirm that realism best explains the success of evolution.

Such is the dialectic between realism and constructivism, which I leave inconclusive. My purpose in providing it is to develop the narrower point that neither realism nor constructivism entails either singularism or multiplism. Singularism is compatible with either realism or constructivism, and multiplism is compatible with either realism or constructivism. Yet, to say that an ontology to qualify as realist or constructivist does not entail either singularism or multiplism, is not to say that one could not formulate a realist type or constructivist type of ontology so that it might entail singularism or multiplism. The point is that a realist or a constructivist ontology need not entail singularism or multiplism. Let us now consider alternative irenic ontologies that combine features of both realism and constructivism. I shall ask of them in turn whether they need entail either singularism or multiplism.

NOTES

1. *Philadelphia Daily News,* Monday, March 31, 1997, 1.
2. John Searle, *The Construction of Social Reality* (New York: Free Press, 1995), 150.
3. Searle, *The Construction of Social Reality,* 155. Emphasis in original.
4. R. G. Collingwood, *An Autobiography* (Oxford: Clarendon, 1939), 44.
5. Karl Popper in ed. David Miller, *Popper Selections* (Princeton, N.J.: Princeton University Press, 1985), 170.
6. Popper, in *Popper Selections,* 222.
7. Ludwig Wittgenstein, *Philosophical Investigations* (Oxford: Basil Blackwell, 1958), 35, 17e.
8. I use Goodman's idea of symbol systems as a cognate of conceptual schemes or languages or the like, in order to contrast the constructivist from the realist view. Goodman's is one of a number of idioms that one might use for such a purpose. Any misgivings one might have specifically about Goodman's way of setting out the constructivist view need not deter our using his idiom as a specimen. Alternatively, following Searle's vocabulary, for example, one might (as I have already done) set out the constructivist's view in terms of representation-dependence.
9. Nelson Goodman, "The Fabrication of Facts," in ed. Jack Meiland and Michael Krausz, *Relativism: Cognitive and Moral* (Notre Dame: Notre Dame University Press, 1982), 21.
10. Nelson Goodman, "Just the Facts, Ma'am," in ed. Michael Krausz, *Relativism: Interpretation and Confrontation* (Notre Dame: Notre Dame University Press, 1989), 83–84.
11. Goodman, "Just the Facts, Ma'am," 84–85.
12. Goodman, "Just the Facts, Ma'am," 81.
13. Goodman, "Just the Facts, Ma'am," 84.
14. Catherine Elgin, *Between the Absolute and the Arbitrary* (Ithaca, N.Y.: Cornell University Press, 1997), 182.
15. Goodman, "Just the Facts, Ma'am," 81.

Chapter Five

Toward a Constructive Realism

I have indicated that according to an initial mapping, four orthodox and heterodox positions were generated by overlapping the distinctions between singularism and multiplism on the one hand, and realism and constructivism on the other hand. Accordingly, since one could coherently adopt the combined positions of singularism–realism, singularism–constructivism, multiplism–realism, or multiplism–constructivism, the interpretive ideals of singularism and multiplism were taken to be detachable from the ontologies of realism and constructivism. As we develop our ramified mapping by considering versions of constructive realism, we should keep in mind that our central concern is to affirm their detachability from singularism and multiplism. It is not, finally, to propound one ontology over another.

In anticipation of our outline of versions of constructive realism—especially *internal* and *external* constructive realism—I rehearse realism and constructivism as they might apply, respectively, to objects, properties, or levels of discourse.

REALISM AND CONSTRUCTIVISM BY OBJECT, PROPERTY, OR LEVEL OF DISCOURSE

Versions of constructive realism may be formulated by (a) ranging realism and constructivism over different sorts of objects, by (b) ranging realism and constructivism over different sorts of properties, or by (c) ranging realism and constructivism over different levels of discourse. I shall comment on these in turn.

(a) The distinction between realism and constructivism is characteristically applied in a global way. That is, "the world" or all of its objects are taken to be either representation-independent or representation-dependent.

51

A global realist holds that all objects are representation-independent. Such a global realism forecloses the possibility that cultural entities, say, might be representation-dependent. In contrast a piecemeal realist might hold that there are some sorts of objects that answer to realism and other sorts of objects answer to constructivism. Accordingly, one might hold that middle-sized objects answer to realism and that certain cultural objects answer to constructivism. One might distinguish representation-independent objects from representation-dependent objects by noting that the former have no history and the latter do. That piecemeal view is what I call constructive realism with respect to objects. According to this view there is no reason for a piecemeal realist to be a global realist.

Yet such an application of realism and constructivism over different kinds of objects might be thought to be vulnerable to the constructivist's reductio of realism. That is, even sticks and stones (as well as cultural entities) are intelligible only in the context of a symbol system in which their representations are nested, that is, one that distinguishes sticks from branches and trees, and one that distinguishes stones from pebbles and boulders. The constructivist's reductio might be taken to tend toward the conclusion that constructivism must be global and that realism cannot be injected in a piecemeal way.

Note that I make no claim that the constructivist reductio is decisive. I say only that one who finds it so may be drawn to recast those objects originally construed in a realist way in a constructivist way.

(b) Alternatively, one might seek to apply realism or constructivism to kinds of *properties* of objects. That is, certain properties of a given object may be thought to answer to a realist construal, and other properties may be thought to answer to a constructivist construal.

Consider three examples to see how realism and constructivism with respect to properties might be applied in a piecemeal way. Consider an electron. Certain of its properties (mass, for example) may be thought to be candidates for a realist treatment, and other properties (position and momentum, for example) may be thought to be candidates for a constructivist treatment. John Bell has corroborated that an electron's position and momentum not only cannot be simultaneously measured, but that electrons do not simultaneously *have* the properties of position or momentum before appropriate setups have been installed. These properties appear to answer to a constructivist's treatment. But it does not follow that there are no electrons independent of experimental setups, since other properties such as mass are not dependent upon experimental setups. More fully, Peter Kosso reports that

> there is no evidence that all properties of a quantum system are indeterminate before they are measured. Things like electric charge, mass, and spin have no Bell-like proofs that give us reason to believe that their classical determinateness is inappropriate to a quantum description. Thus, the part of the first premise of

the Copenhagen interpretation that claims that *no* determinate classical values can be applied to a quantum system is an overstatement, misleading at best, downright false at worst.[1]

Kosso summarizes his view this way.

Proof that entities lack some properties is not a reason to think that they lack all properties, and it does not threaten their existence or reality.[2]

In other words, when impressed with the constructivism of certain properties of a thing we should not slide into a global "property" constructivism. Kosso's is a fair warning. At the same time, we should ask, are even such properties as an electron's charge, mass, and spin vulnerable to the constructivist's reductio? Even if mass, for example, were the same for all electrons, could it not answer to the constructivist construal? And does this not tend toward the conclusion (again) that constructivism must be global, thus disallowing a piecemeal injection of realism?

One might be tempted to say that, with respect to the identity of an electron, mass is an essential property, but its position and momentum are nonessential properties. Accordingly, some of the properties of the electron answer to a realist construal and others to a constructivist construal.

Note that an electron should not be treated as "just another kind of thing." Harré suggests why this is the case. He emphasizes that a logical subject need not be a substantive entity.

Why are electrons candidates for the role of logical subject to which the elementary negative charge, spin, inertial mass and so on are ascribed? Electrons express themselves in tracks, spatially distinct trajectories. At first glance they seem to be just another kind of material thing. But since they cannot be labeled the numerical identity of electrons through all kinds of encounters is problematic. Their identity conditions are more like those for sums of money, cups of sugar borrowed and returned, than they are like those kinds of material objects which can be distinctively and uniquely labeled.

Quark identity is like pain identity. Quarks are expressed in jets, streams of particles whose origin is in quark interactions, so that we can say that to be a quark of a certain kind is to be disposed to give rise to just this jet of just these kinds of particles. Quarks cannot be juxtaposed for comparison, neither in past and present encounters nor across physical phenomena. They are known only in their expression in contexts which will elicit their powers. To be just this quark is to afford just this jet of particles.

Why should quarks be candidates for the role of logical subjects to which causal powers are ascribed? A logical subject in physics must have a spatio-temporal location, though it need not be punctiform. Many logical subjects have spatio-temporal trajectories, though this does not seem to be a necessary condition for the role of bearer of properties and, as discursively represented, as a subject of predication.[3]

Consider a second example of how realism and constructivism with respect to properties might apply in a piecemeal way. A particular violin embodies some properties that appear to answer to a realist treatment and others that appear to answer to a constructivist treatment. Fred Oster, a Philadelphia dealer and appraiser of fine instruments, was engaged to appraise the Stradivarius of the late renowned violinist and pedagogue, Josef Gingold. Oster opined that the instrument was "a mess," for it had been repaired often and the varnish had been done over several times. Of course, it was a Stradivarius and for that reason alone it was valuable. But Oster said that it was especially valuable because it had belonged to Gingold. Here we have a physical object that, under special circumstances, has powers to produce certain sounds. Second, it is one of a class of instruments made by a consummate master. Third, it is further valued on account of its ownership by an esteemed violinist and pedagogue. The instrument's value depends in part upon the value assigned to it by pertinent practitioners in light of received norms. The object did not "have" special value before the assignment of value. The violin had different properties before and after the ownership by Gingold. The self-same violin *became* more valuable. While (in piecemeal fashion) the assignment of value seems to be hospitable to a constructivist treatment, at first blush it appears that the physical properties of the violin being able to produce certain sounds answers to a realist construal. That is, certain properties would seem to answer to realism and other properties would seem to answer to constructivism.

Yet even those properties that appear to answer to realism might be vulnerable to the constructivist's reductio, namely, those properties cannot be made intelligible independent of some symbol system. (Again, I do not claim that the constructivist's reductio is conclusive.) In such a case, even the physical properties of the violin could be made sense of only within some symbol system that distinguishes those properties capable of producing pertinent sounds from other contrasting properties. As in the first example, constructivism with respect to properties would seem to apply in a global way only. But in the absence of the global applicability of the constructivist's reductio, some properties might answer to a realist construal and others to a constructivist construal.

Consider a third example of an object whose different properties might be treated in a realist way and a constructivist way. Consider the example of a country. Standardly, a country is taken to require a land (being practice-independent) and to be ordained as sovereign by pertinent international bodies (being practice-dependent). No doubt, there are numerous cases where different peoples or nations struggle in different ways to obtain either condition. The point is that, paradigmatically, a country requires both these sorts of properties. A global realist with respect to properties might say that the landedness of the country answers to realism and that its sovereignty also answers to realism. The piecemealist may say that the landedness answers to realism and that the sovereignty answers to constructivism. Either way, the landedness is taken to answer to realism. Yet even here a constructivist might hold that, although it might appear that landedness answers to realism, it too—along with sovereignty—answers to constructivism. Landedness cannot be made sense of independently of some symbol systems in which it is nested. But (again) in the absence of the global applicability of the constructivist's reductio, some properties might answer to a realist construal and others to a constructivist construal.

(c) We have considered the strategy of parceling realism and constructivism, first over types of objects, and second over kinds of properties. Now let us consider parceling realism and constructivism according to level of discourse. This way of doing so will be especially pertinent in our treatment of constructive realism in chapters 6 through 9.

A realist and a constructivist might well agree that *at the first order* there is a distinction between certain sorts of objects or properties, that some objects or properties are representation-independent and others are representation-dependent. But they may well disagree *at the second order* about how to construe the agreed-upon first-order distinction. That is, while it is one thing to claim that we can distinguish between objects or properties at the first order, it is another thing to claim at the second order that the first-order distinction itself is real or constructed.

A second-order realist holds that the distinction between representation-independence versus representation-dependence reflects a found (versus made) difference. In contrast, a second-order constructivist holds that the distinction amounts to a made difference. The second-order constructivist holds that any distinction between the real and the constructed (or between the real and the unreal, or between the real and the imaginary) at the first order, for example, is subtended under a second-order constructivism. The second-order constructivist holds that the distinction between practice-independence and practice-dependence (or representation-independence and representation-dependence) is itself constructed at the second order. At that second order the distinction is representation-dependent or practice-dependent. On this view, one might well parcel first-order objects or properties according to a criterion of representation-independence or representation-dependence while the criterion itself is understood to be constructed at the second order. The first-order distinction would be subtended under a second-order constructivism.

The difference between second-order realism and second-order constructivism may be seen when contrasting a mountain with a country. A second-order realist would distinguish these at the first order by noting that a mountain is what it is independently of any representation. And a country is what it is in virtue of its being represented in one way or another. A second-order realist would affirm that the distinction between real and constructed is a real distinction, itself being representation-independent. In contrast, the second-order constructivist would distinguish between the mountain and the country on the grounds that both are constructed in different ways, because the very distinction between real and constructed is itself constructed. While the second-order realist can be realist with respect to some or all first-order objects, the constructivist must be constructivist with respect to all objects. This still allows the constructivist—within his or her subtended logical space—to distinguish nonintentional from intentional first-order objects, so long as nonintentional objects themselves are taken to answer to a second-order constructivist construal.

The challenge facing second-order realism is that it must make itself immune from the constructivist's *reductio*, for the constructivist may counter that, say, even physical objects or properties of sticks and stones are intelligible only in terms of some symbol system. The challenge is to make coherent the thought that the distinction between representation-independence and representation-dependence is itself representation-independent.

In turn, the challenge facing second-order constructivism is that it must, in constructivist terms, account for what appears to be first-order representation-independent objects, while keeping those objects' apparent "resilience" as an explanatory datum. Further, any apparent difference between real and constructed objects must be seen as a difference between types of constructed objects. The second-order constructivist is committed to holding that, finally, all first-order objects are representation-dependent, that finally they are constructed.

TOWARD A CONSTRUCTIVE REALISM

Given the above sketch of realism and constructivism with respect to objects, properties, and levels of discourse, we are now in a position to formulate versions of constructive realism. The realist and constructivist may agree that there is a difference in kind between certain sorts of first-order objects. And, they may even agree that what they both refer to as "real" objects is constructed *if,* that is, the realist be allowed a shift in nomenclature that would countenance his or her positing *something* (not yet ordained as real) beyond the symbol system. Such a shift would allow that "real objects" are subtended under a constructivist rubric, so long as "real objects" are not identified with what may be presystematically posited as *there*. The result of such a shift would allow the realist to legitimately ask such questions as, "Where do the real objects come from? And what pre-systematic 'materia' is there for the construction of 'real' things?" Such a shift would disallow that that which is presystematically there consists of real objects. Real objects would be internal to representing systems.

Were the realist to agree to this shift of nomenclature, we might collect our realist and constructivist under a rubric that we may dub as "constructive realist." Yet the remaining difference between them would be understood in terms of a distinction between *internal* and *external* constructive realism. The internal constructive realist would say that there can be no appeal to any-thing—real or otherwise—that precedes the symbol system. The external constructive realist would say that, although they cannot be countenanced as real objects, some presystematic "materia" needs to be appealed to in order to account for the construction of real objects. The internal constructive realist holds that there is nothing *there* or we can make no sense of the claim that there is something *there* outside symbol systems. In contrast, the external constructive realist agrees that real objects are not outside symbol systems, or one cannot make sense of the claim that real objects are outside symbol systems. But this claim does not prohibit one's positing that there is something *there* outside of symbol systems that constitutes the "materia" from which real objects are constituted within symbol systems.

We may anticipate some varieties of constructive realism to come in chapters 6 through 9. Harré attempts to capture the motivating intuition of realism, namely that there is something out *there* independent of our beliefs and conceptions. But he affirms that what can be said about what is there cannot include real objects or their properties, for real objects are constructed. External constructive realist Harré holds that the real objects and their properties are constructions and are relative to constructing systems. Yet he affirms that what is *there* has the power to produce phenomena relative to a given apparatus. Notice that Harré's external constructive realism does not entail (though it is compatible with) the view that there is an *alternativity* of ways in which, as he also says, phenomena are "afforded." That is, a singularist could well agree with Harré's external constructive realism and resist his rider of alternativity.

In turn, Harrison and Hanna's external constructive realism (or "relative realism" as they call it) subtends real objects under a second-order constructivism. Harrison and Hanna recommend that the classical picture of reference that holds that referents must be independent of interpretive practices should be jettisoned. Reference does not require external realism. Yet what is out *there* has, as they say, "the power to deliver a verdict of true or false on judgments formulated in terms of the things and features constructed in terms of given practices." The rejection of direct realism and the transcendental theory of reference does not entail that there is no viable account of the real and of reference. Yet Harrison and Hanna *also* hold that there is no single right language in terms of which especially human phenomena can be understood. This rider of the alternativity of language is independent of the first ontological claim of constructive realism. That is, a singularist could embrace Harrison and Hanna's constructive realism and at the same time deny that there is an alternativity of languages in terms of which especially human phenomena can be understood. In other words,

Harrison and Hanna's rider of alternativity is logically detachable from their first claim of constructive realism. Harrison and Hanna's constructive realism entails neither singularism nor multiplism.

In turn, while Margolis's internal constructive realism subtends real objects under a second-order constructivism, he denies Harré's and Harrison and Hanna's claim that what is out there can be spoken of even in terms of powers to "afford phenomena" or "to deliver a verdict of true or false." A singularist might agree with Margolis's internal constructive realism. But Margolis adds the rider of alternativity in his assertion that there may be a multiplicity of admissible and incongruent interpretations of cultural objects. I do not say that the rider of alternativity is false, only that it is detachable from the ontology of constructive realism, whether internal or external.

Let us not lose sight of our overall purpose. In the following chapters I shall offer versions of constructive realism to ramify the landscape of ontological theories and to show how these ontologies are detachable from the interpretive ideals of singularism and multiplism. I shall argue that both the internal and external constructive realist ontologies make real objects parasitic of some symbol system. But their doing so does not mandate that there is an *alternativity* of symbol systems. Thus, the ontologies are detachable from the associated rider of alternativity. So understood, the pertinent versions of constructive realism entail neither singularism nor multiplism. Put otherwise, both the singularist and the multiplist might accept designated versions of constructive realism, so long as they remain neutral as to whether there is an alternativity of admissible symbol systems. But even the alternativity of admissible symbol systems still does not entail multiplism, for such alternativity is also compatible with singularism, where, that is, different objects of interpretation answer to different admissible symbol systems.

NOTES

1. Peter Kosso, *Appearance and Reality: An Introduction to the Philosophy of Physics* (New York: Oxford University Press, 1998), 161.
2. Kosso, *Appearance and Reality: An Introduction to the Philosophy of Physics,* 154.
3. Rom Harré, "Is There a Basic Ontology for the Physical Sciences?" *Dialectica,* 51, Fasc. 1 (1997), 33, 34.

Chapter Six

Constructive Realists (I): Harré

CONCERNING ALTERNATIVITY AND IDEALITY

The rider of alternativity entails neither singularism nor multiplism, for singularism and multiplism both require that it is a given *single* object of interpretation that is being addressed by one interpretation (for the singularist) or by more than one competing interpretation (for the multiplist). And the alternativity of symbol systems or conceptual schemes is compatible with but does not entail there being a *single* object of interpretation.

Alternativity holds that there is a diversity of taxonomic classifications, systems of counting, conceptual schemes, or the like. While characteristically the diversity of such schemes is taken to address a common self-same object, there may be such a diversity of conceptual schemes without the pertinent commonality. Alternativity alone is compatible with either multiplism or singularism. In the course of our discussion about representative versions of constructive realism we should be alert to whether the claim of alternativity uncritically slides into the claim of multiplism on account of an unsupported assumption that the alternative schemes address a single self-same object of interpretation.

In chapter 3, I noted that Thom holds that there are different ways in which a "further object" might be represented. In the present chapter I shall note that Harré holds that there are diverse ways to "afford" an object. In Harré, alternativity expresses itself in the claim that, depending upon the adopted world-apparatus setup, the world-stuff affords phenomena, *and there are numerous world-apparatus setups*. And in chapter 8 I shall note that Putnam holds that there are alternative ways of counting, leaving it open what objects are thereby counted. For Putnam, alternativity expresses itself in the claim that the number of entities in the universe depends upon one's system of counting *and there are numerous such systems*. And in chapter 9 I shall note that Margolis holds that an object may be imputed differently. For Margolis, alternativity expresses itself in the claim that interpretations impute properties and change objects of interpretation, *and there are numerous such interpretations*. Yet given alternativity alone, it remains open whether there is one self-same thing that is being represented, afforded, counted, or imputed. Indeed, one might well concede alternativity and still hold that that which is represented, afforded, counted, or imputed has no determinate number independently of a pertinent scheme. The mere fact that there are differences in the way one conceptualizes does not entail that what is alternatively conceptualized is one common object. The pertinent object(s) may be common, uncommon, or it may be undecidable whether it is common or not. In sum, alternativity is compatible with singularism or multiplism, or with the undecidability of either of these. So the ontologies of realism, constructivism, and constructive realism which assume alternativity—without a supplementing account of sameness or commonality of their object of interpretation—are neutral with respect to singularism and multiplism.

I refer to alternativity as a "rider" of constructive realism. For constructive realism is formulable without alternativity. That is, a constructive realist might hold that there is no diversity of eligible conceptual schemes, that instead there is only one proper way to construct pertinent objects. A singularist might insist that there is one proper world-apparatus with which to unite the world-stuff in affording a phenomenon (contra Harré); or there is only one proper way to count entities of the universe (contra Putnam); or there is only one proper way to impute properties to a given object (contra Margolis). In short, from the fact that objects of interpretation are constructed it does not follow that there is an alternativity of modes for such construction. Let us now consider various versions of constructive realism.

HARRÉ

Harré embraces a kind of constructive realism in that he holds that there is a "world-stuff" (or "glub" as he also sometimes calls it), independent of interpretive activity. But ascribable properties are "afforded" in the context of experiential or experimental "setups." That is, the ascribability of particular properties to the world is interpretation-dependent.

Harré draws upon suggestions from physicist Niels Bohr and psychologist J. J. Gibson in holding that the world is indefinitely complex and capable of displaying a huge variety of aspects of itself, depending on the way that it is approached and experimented with. None of the actual properties in which the world reveals itself can be known to be identical with the properties of the world as it is independently of the situations and setups in which different aspects of its character are manifested. All we ever experience are effects of certain powers and dispositions of "world-apparatus" or "world-people" combinations. All we can properly ascribe to the world are powers to produce this or that effect in us or in our apparatus. Consequently, all we say about the world must take a conditional form, namely, *if* certain conditions are fulfilled *then* the world will (or could) manifest itself in this or that way. The track in a cloud chamber, for example, is a manifestation of electronhood that is available to human beings only in the context of that cloud chamber. It is the world and the cloud chamber that has a disposition to display itself as electron-tracks. What of the electrons that we picture as causing the tracks? They too are but "affordances" of the total setup. (Harré borrows the term from Gibson.) It follows that the way the world is manifested to human beings depends upon which instrument is being used to bring forth that disposition. For Harré, there is no point to asking what is the complete and determinate nature of an object independent of "world-apparatus" or "world-people" complexes.

Harré asks where the "world-stuff" that is made determinate in experimental setup comes from. He asks:

How can we have real causal powers which are nevertheless sensitive to the fact that the dispositions with which they endow physical particulars are relative to the particular apparatus in which they are manifested?

Bohr's solution to this problem, though he might not have put it in quite this way, is based on the thesis that at the centre of the scientific enterprise are beings he calls "phenomena." Phenomena arise from and are produced in a characteristic kind of interaction between the world and an apparatus of a specific sort. For example, the *entity* we call an electron is an aspect of electronic *phenomena* that are brought into being by a certain kind of apparatus bringing out something from the world. . . . Bohr argued that the assumption that an apparatus is a transparent window on reality is not acceptable *in general*.

It follows that we cannot infer that because our apparatus in interaction with the world affords electrons, it has revealed something that would have existed had the apparatus not been switched on. Yet we do want to say that, in some way or other, what we do in physics with an apparatus tells us something about the world—but what does it tell us? Clearly, if the Bohrian view is in general correct, then it cannot be telling us what the dispositions of the world are. . . . There is a refinement of the concept of a disposition that comes from psychology of perception developed by J.J. Gibson . . . , namely, the 'affordance.' An affordance is a disposition the display of which occurs in circumstances created by or relevant to human interests. For example a pair of scissors affords cutting or the ice on a lake in the winter affords walking. The human element in the spelling out of affordances can never be eliminated. Applying this idea in physics we have the claim that the world affords electrons just in combination with a particular kind of apparatus. Ice affords walking so long as I do not have my pet elephant with me. What the causal powers of the world affords experimenters will depend on the apparatus employed. . . . The world has the power to afford electron phenomena when in indissoluble union with instances of a certain class of apparatus.[1]

Harré says:

> In the Bohrian philosophy of physics, physical theories concretely realized in apparatus shape up the generic stuff of the world, which we could call the 'glub,' into the causally structured and spatially and temporally differentiated world of phenomena, which our apparatus, in interaction with the world, affords us. The apparatus cannot be subtracted from the equation to leave the world pure and simple, because it is the organizing power of the apparatus through which phenomena are brought into being from the 'glub.' In a similar way the Kantian schematisms cannot be factored out of the empirical world, leaving behind the noumenal sources of the sensory flux.[2]

Harré says further:

> electrons exist *as such,* that is as spatio-temporally individuatable entities, only in the context of the apparatus/world complex. *They* are brought into being in the apparatus. If we set up and activate another kind of apparatus, we will bring wave-like phenomena into existence. . . . The phenomena are afforded by an apparatus/world complex only if the world has the power to generate such beings when intimately interconnected with the relevant apparatus. The world affords electrons in just this kind of apparatus, the world affords waves in just that kind of apparatus, and so on.[3]

And finally:

> This allows us to say there are properties of the world that are such that their empirical content is always given by their mode of manifestation.[4]

To the construction-independent world-stuff, Harré does ascribe though at least one property, namely that in union with pertinent setups the world-stuff has the power to afford empirical manifestations in one form or another. The world-stuff is taken to be representation-independent lacking in empirical content, yet when in union in a world-apparatus its empirical content emerges. Here is how Harré describes the emergence of empirical content.

> Bohr saw that the performing of an experiment created an 'internal' relation between the material apparatus as used by the experimenter and the material stuff with which it interacted. The relation is 'internal' in that the apparatus, when in use, brings into being a state of affairs which, though it is the manifestation of a real disposition or tendency or natural power of the world stuff, is not just a manifestation of those dispositions. The form that manifestation takes is shaped by the apparatus and the way it is used. The indissoluble totality of the apparatus-world manifestation is what Bohr meant by phenomenon. It makes no sense to ask "What would an electron be like if there were no electron-displaying apparatus?" since the world disposition in question is only displayed *as an electron* in that kind of set-up. There is nothing subjectivist or relativist about this idea. 'Electrons' are relational properties of some well-defined types of apparatus-world ensembles.

We shall say . . . that a certain kind of apparatus-world ensemble *affords* relevant category of entities, properties, processes and so on to some instrument or
observer or manipulator.[5]

Let us collect Harré's salient claims. For him physics tells us something
about the world. Yet we cannot strip away the contribution of the apparatus
and ascribe pure powers to the world. The phenomenon of the electron qua
electron is brought into being by a certain kind of apparatus bringing out
something from the world. The entity is not a parcel of the world but a particular apparatus-world complex. The world *affords* electrons just in combination with a particular kind of apparatus. What the causal powers of the
world affords experimenters will depend on the apparatus employed. The
world has the power to afford electron phenomena when in indissoluble union
with an apparatus. While an apparatus in interaction with the world affords
electrons, one cannot infer that it has revealed something that would have existed had the apparatus not been switched on. An affordance is a disposition
the display of which occurs in circumstances created by or relevant to human
interests, and this human element can never be eliminated. Synoptically, we
may put Harré's view this way. The world-stuff in indissoluble union with apparatus constitutes a "phenomenon," which in turn affords an object that has
empirical content and may answer to interpretations.

Harré's constructive realism seeks to satisfy the concern that without something *there* (the world-stuff) to which to ascribe properties, it remains myste-
rious what interpretations might finally be about. Yet the paradox is that, preceding world-apparatus complexes, properties as such cannot be ascribed at
all. Harré can say nothing about the world-stuff except (paradoxically) that it
has the disposition to be manifested in certain ways.

Notice that Harré's world-stuff can do no methodological or distributive
work, only the philosophical work of making sense of the world-apparatus
complex that afford phenomena. At the same time, the world-stuff is not denumerable. It is not countable. One cannot say that it, singularly, is that which
interpretations are about. Even were one to say that *indirectly* (as in Thom's
"further object") interpretations are about the world-stuff, its singularity
could not be assumed—not because, again, it might be multiple, but rather because it is not countable at all. Countability might obtain at the level of
"world-apparatus" complexes, but not at the level of the world-stuff. It is only
at the level of world-apparatus that an object as such can be constituted as
countable. The world-stuff cannot be differentiated as to number. So the question as to whether the world-stuff is one or more cannot arise. Thus, as regards interpretations of the world-stuff, neither singularism nor multiplism
can be affirmed.

If, as Harré's theory suggests, the world-stuff cannot be said to be singular-
or-multiple it might be better to say that, with respect to the world-stuff, singularism and multiplism are *undecidable*. This still allows that singularism or

multiplism might apply after phenomena have been constituted and individuated in the context of a world-apparatus.

Further, Harré conjoins his ontological claim about the construction of phenomena in world-apparatus complexes, with the rider of alternativity. That claim is that there may be a diversity of setups. But this conjunctive claim still does not entail multiplism, for it is an open question whether candidate interpretations address the same object. The claim that phenomena reside in world-apparatus complexes does not by itself entail multiplism. Indeed, a singularist might agree that phenomena reside in world-apparatus complexes but still assert that there is one and only one admissible apparatus that should be coupled with the world-stuff. Harré's claim that phenomena obtain in world-apparatus complexes is *logically distinct* from the rider of alternativity, and the rider of alternativity mandates neither singularism nor multiplism. In this way, Harré's ontology of constructive realism remains neutral with respect to singularism and multiplism.

NOTES

1. Rom Harré, "Is There a Basic Ontology for the Physical Sciences?" *Dialectica,* 51, Fasc. 1 (1997), 24–25.
2. Harré, "Is There a Basic Ontology for the Physical Sciences?" 25.
3. Harré, "Is There a Basic Ontology for the Physical Sciences?" 26.
4. Harré, "Is There a Basic Ontology for the Physical Sciences?" 27.
5. Rom Harré, "A Realist Theory of Properties," in ed. Jerrold L. Aronson, Rom Harré, and Eileen Cornell Way, *Realism Rescued* (Chicago: Open Court, 1995), 179–81.

Chapter Seven

Constructive Realists (II): Harrison and Hanna, and Wallner

HARRISON AND HANNA'S RELATIVE REALISM

We find an undecidability about the sameness of object(s) of interpretation addressed by otherwise competing interpretations in the ontologies of Bernard Harrison and Patricia Hanna. In their forthcoming book, *Word and World: Reference and Linguistic Convention*, Harrison and Hanna oppose a traditional picture of realism that they call referential realism. They advance an alternative view that they call relative realism.[1]

Harrison and Hanna characterize referential realism as the view that there is one kind of link between language and some aspect or element of Reality "whose existence is prior to and independent of language."[2] In its place relative realism invokes three elements: word, world, and practice. Harrison and Hanna say:

> What actually relates language to reality . . . is better conceived as a two-level process of engagement, or embedding: at the first level the engagement, or embedding, of linguistic expressions in practices; at the second level the engagement, or embedding, of practices in the matrix of natural conditions and circumstances, in and with respect to which they are carried on.[3]

In our terms relative realism is a kind of external constructive realism. That is, it assumes that there is a world of some kind. While there is no direct way of relating word to world, it does so via pertinent practices that "engage" or "embed" the world. The notion of "engage" or "embed" is critical. Harrison and Hanna say that

> all talk of what an expression "designates" or "refers to" is in the end merely a shorthand way of talking about the manner in which that expression engages with, or is involved in, some practice or other. . . . The supposed *entities* in the

case would then dissolve, not quite into thin air, but into modes of engagement. The mode of engagement of an expression with a practice, now, is clearly not part of the furniture of the natural, "extralinguistic world." On the contrary, it is quintessentially a work of human invention, as much a fabrication of ingenuity in the forging of convention as, say, the Petrarchan Sonnet Form or the rules of golf. It would follow, in other words, that when we speak of the entities referred to or designated by expressions we speak, so far as we speak of anything at all, of fabrications of the mind.[4]

Notice that Harrison and Hanna take the supposed entities to dissolve "not quite into thin air." That means, I take it, that they are not prepared to deny the practice-independent element that becomes embedded in practices. But they shift the attention of reference from such a presumed element to that which is a human invention, that which is a fabrication of the mind.

Harrison and Hanna emphasize that the bearing of language

is a function . . . of the modes of engagement of practices with the world. A practice just *is* a mode of engaging with the contents of reality, as they present themselves to creatures with the physical constitution and perceptual powers of human beings.[5]

Their view is pointedly expressed when they address the idea of truth conditions.

Truth-conditions, like concepts, are not to be encountered in nature. The truth-conditions of an utterance U, and thus the status of U as . . . the kind of utterance with respect to which it is intelligible to raise the issue of truth or falsity, can only be determined relative to some means of singling out, among the infinity of features and aspects presented by what Quine felicitously dubs "the passing show" those which are truth-relevant to U; and that means can only be provided by the enmeshing of U in some practice, some language game. And, since grasping the reference of an expression is in part a matter of grasping the truth conditions attaching to sentences in which it can occur, the concept of reference also will turn out, if we are correct, to be dependent upon and derivative from the prior notion of a practice.[6]

With respect to reference, practice takes priority over any presumed practice-independent entity. For, presumably, the entity is already presented as something that is embedded in practice, one whose features and aspects have been singled out for presentation in the way it has. Accordingly, the very idea of a practice-independent entity can have no functional content. It is in this sense that Harrison and Hanna say that a word is "always already connected to the world."

Harrison and Hanna underscore that concepts are practice-relative when they say that their account

holds that concepts are relative to practices: that what concepts a natural language honours is determined not by the nature of things but by the specific range of practices which enter into the constitution of that particular natural language.[7]

Notice that the claim that concepts are practice-relative is compatible with the assertion either that (a) there is one privileged set of practices to which they are relative, or (b) there is an alternativity of such practices. This is a version of the thesis of alternativity. Harrison and Hanna opt for the latter option when they say that their account

> contends also that, since no limit can be set in principle either to human purposes or to the practices which human inventiveness may devise in their service, so no limit can be set to the invention of new concepts.[8]

Presumably that alternativity is what makes their relative realism a *relative* realism. Yet the question arises, in the absence of a practice-independent entity, how one can judge whether a practice-dependent concept is more or less adequate than another. Without such a practice-independent entity it might be thought that one could well move from one practice-dependent concept to another without any grounding between them. Put otherwise, if there is a slide from one practice-dependent concept to another, without something that grounds that of which the concepts address, it would appear to be impossible to gauge whether one concept was more or less adequate. Under these conditions an innocuous pluralism might obtain—where different concepts address different things. Competition between concepts would not operate. (Under these conditions perhaps a better label for the resulting situation would be "pluralist realist" rather than "relative realist.")

Harrison and Hanna affirm that there is no external common grounding when they say

> that the structure and content of the canons of rationality composing such spaces can be fully understood in terms of the modes of engagement of practices with reality, without invoking any further "grounding" or "justification" external to the practice and its mode of engagement with the world.[9]

As a vestige of referential realism one might be tempted to hold that the practice-independent element should play an adequational role. But according to Harrison and Hanna, it could not adjudicate between contesting concepts. One could not say what those concepts were meant to distribute over, for the practice-independent element (or its features or aspects) would not have already been "singled out." That is why, after all, Harrison and Hanna insist that such an element cannot count as a truth condition. Truth conditions are always and only embedded in practices.

Harrison and Hanna countenance that there is a world independent of practices, but such a world can have no adequational role. Yet there is an embedded world, one embedded in pertinent practices. And that embedded world may well perform all the usual functions of adequacy, including that of distributing between true and false claims. Harrison and Hanna respond to this challenge when they say:

> it is as possible to be mistaken about what concepts correspond to reality as it is to be mistaken about what judgments correspond to the facts. The holder of the Correspondence Theory of Meaning, in other words, does not regard the phlogiston theory as an erroneous theory of combustion framed in terms of a well-formed concept, "phlogiston." For him what is wrong with the theory is not merely that its judgments fail to match up to reality; the concepts, or some of them, in which that theory is formulated fail to match up to reality as well.[10]

By this Harrison means that

> the "adequation" of one system of concepts relative to another comes about through processes operating INTERNALLY to the total system of practices taken together with their modes of insertion into the world. Physics abandons the concept of phlogiston, that is, not because it discovers that there is nothing "in the world" which "phlogiston" picks out, but because a view of the nature of combustion in which there is no place for such a concept turns out to provide a better explanation of the phenomena, "better" here being explicated in terms of the goals of physics as a practice seeking types of explanation yielding certain specific benefits and susceptible to revision through certain sorts of experimental procedure; given also that the sense physicists have of what those "certain" benefits and procedures may amount to may change over time, again through processes operating internally to the practice of physics. (The "relation between physics and the world," that is, is a relation between the PRACTICE of physics and the world, not between the CONCEPTUAL VOCABULARY of physics, taken concept-by-concept, and the world.)[11]

If interpretations may compete about a common object of interpretation, it must be of an object taken in a certain way, that is, embedded in a certain way. And the extent to which multiplism, for example, may obtain depends upon the commonality of the practice-embedded object that the rival interpretations address. If Harrison and Hanna are right, the condition of multiplism obtains "internally to the total system of practices, taken together with their modes of insertion into the world." Thus the world as such cannot provide individuated "objects" that otherwise would provide necessary grounds for commonality of that which competing interpretations would address.

In sum, as in previous ontological accounts, from the claim that the only functional worlds are practice-embedded worlds, the rider that there are many practice-embedded worlds is not entailed. That is an independent claim. Further, as in Harré, no conditions of individuation of "pre-praxial" elements are forthcoming, so with respect to them neither singularism nor multiplism can apply.

WALLNER'S CONSTRUCTIVE REALISM

Let us now add to our collection of constructive realists by considering Fritz Wallner. I have used the phrase "constructive realism" as a heading for a number of views that collect elements of realism and constructivism. It is important to mention Wallner's theory in this discussion because in German-speaking philosophical circles it is he who has made the phrase constructive realism well-known. Wallner's constructive realism is of an external kind. He holds that, although *environment* precedes the constructed real order, *reality* is interpretation-dependent.[12]

In his book *How to Deal with Science if You Care for Other Cultures: Constructive Realism in the Intercultural World,* Wallner sketches his *constructive realism* in response to a general recognition, as he puts it, that

> the central method of the Geisteswissenschaften—interpretation—is becoming a leading method in the natural sciences. Therefore in a reversal of the relationship between natural sciences and Geisteswissenschaften, the natural sciences are compelled to take a closer look at the methods of the Geisteswissenschaften.[13]

Wallner sketches his constructive realism by defining several cognate pairs of notions in distinctive ways. They include describing and fitting, reality and environment, given world and constructed reality, mastering nature and understanding the world, Wirklichkeit (environment) and Realität (reality), microworlds and scientific reality, and others.

To start with, Wallner notes that, contrary to metaphysical realist accounts, natural scientists do not *describe* a practice-independent world. Rather:

> The real work in natural science is extracting some information by applying specific technical means, putting this information into a theoretical framework, checking it by computer, taking out the results, and then you have a formal system of propositions, which is, in this very special context, fitting or not-fitting. There is no description, there is just a question of fitting.[14]

Thus Wallner restricts the range of what can be known to what is constructed. He says:

> Using the word "construction" we are replacing the conviction that science is describing the world. Constructive Realism is fiercely doubting this common conviction. . . . For getting knowledge it is necessary to integrate something into one's linguistic frame, i.e. to translate it. If you are not able to translate a language of description then you don't understand it. Thus, translation is the point of proof for understanding.[15]

Wallner infers, then, that the objects of scientific activity are not given objects but artificial objects or constructed objects. He says that

> very few scientists would disagree that the objects of scientific activity are not given objects. Rather they are highly artificial objects and result from complicated scientific and technical activities. These *artificial objects are held together by a framework which itself is invented freely.*[16]

On the artificiality of the objects of science, Wallner continues:

> Science in this understanding is not describing the given world. Science is describing a small artificial world which has specific qualities, and the connection between qualities is described by so called natural laws.[17]

Wallner links the ideas of construction, microworld, and phenomena. He takes the artificial objects of science to have been constructed in the context of a framework, the collection of such objects constituting a microworld that allows us to master phenomena. He says:

> In our context, *constructions means that scientists are arranging information by the help of a framework, which is governing the data.* Nothing else is meant with the notion "to construct a microworld." Having constructed a microworld, we are able to master a specific group of phenomena. But still there is no knowledge at this point. You have just got the ability to solve problems.[18]

The question arises as to what scientific practice is *about*. What does it refer to? For Wallner it is not about a practice-independent world. It is about a microworld. Accordingly, he holds that it is about Reality, but Reality is now defined in terms of the microworld and not about a practice-independent order. Thus, he says:

> We have to admit that *science is directed to something which is in some sense without nature.* Reality is the systematical togetherness of microworlds that mankind—at a specific point in time—has elaborated.[19]

And Wallner asserts that:

> The totality of microworlds is reality, or scientific reality. Therefore reality is always relative to a point of historical development.[20]

Wallner contrasts the "given world" or "the environment" with "constructed reality." He says:

> Still there is no good argument that there is no "given world." But the given world must have a different function in the life of human beings than (constructed) reality. With the given world we are connected by life. The given world

is never doubted. For reality, this is not the case. In experimenting with our constructions we have some degree of freedom. If we mess up with the given world, however, we risk our lives. The given world is the world we are living with, both in the sense of biology and in the sense of culture. Therefore a good term for these aspects is "environment," as this term is stressing the aspects of working together, of mutual influence. If you adopt this conceptional terminological difference between reality and environment, then you become able to tell the *difference between mastering nature and understanding the world.*[21]

Wallner contrasts reality with environment in this way:

In German, two words for "reality" exist. We will refer to "Realität" as reality and to "Wirklichkeit" as environment. . . . we distinguish . . . between *two types of reality:* we understand by *"Wirklichkeit" (environment) the world we are living with;* i.e. the world which is pre-supposed to our perceptions and to our processes of life. *"Realität" (reality), the world we are living in,* means our cognitive world, being the result of a process of construction. . . . It rather introduces the differentiation between the world we are living in as environment and the constructed world of our cognition as reality.[22]

Wallner connects the notion of environment to mastery and the notion of knowledge to constructed reality. He says:

The environment cannot be understood. We can only master environment with the help of our constructions of reality. If they serve us well for gaining control over the environment, we keep them. If they don't, we discard them. When it comes to knowledge, however, we can only refer to reality, i.e. to what we have constructed.[23]

Wallner restricts the possibility of understanding to constructed microworlds. The environment beyond microworlds cannot be understood, although it may be controlled via our construction of reality, which is to say via the construction of microworlds. Wallner says:

the environment cannot be understood. We can gain control, however, over the environment by our constructions of reality.[24]

With respect to our knowledge we can understand only what we have constructed. For such scientific constructions we have chosen the name "microworlds."[25]

For Wallner the question of the ontology of the scientific object follows rather than precedes its construction. He says:

in constructing a scientific object you need not and you cannot decide its ontological status. To start with the constructed object is ontologically undefined. (From this point of view we can see the importance of interpretation for scientific objects—for without any interpretation it is impossible to decide what a scientific object is anyway.) When we have determined the ontological structure of an object after its construction, then it becomes (scientific) reality. In other words, it is decided by our free interpretation, what the objects are which we give meaning.[26]

Finally, in a method Wallner calls strangification, he suggests that we compare different constructs of our cognitive reality and in so doing we "leave" the reality of those constructs thereby transforming reality to environment. Wallner says:

> *empirical control of theoretical constructs represents nothing but the comparison between two (different) constructs (of our cognitive reality).* Thereby we do not give up principally the relation to environment; the relation to environment is rather indirect. If we compare two different constructs (of reality), we "leave" reality; we are testing to what extent reality endures beyond the correlations of our constructions. Stated another way we could formulate: By making use of empirical control, we are applying a strangification "transforming reality to environment."[27]

In sum, Wallner takes the real to be coextensive with microworlds, which is to say it is coextensive with constructed objects. This qualifies Wallner's view as a constructive realist in our sense. Yet, Wallner is no idealist, for there is an order beyond what he takes to be the real, and that is the environment. This qualifies Wallner's view as an external constructive realist.

According to Wallner, while singularism or multiplism may obtain between an interpretation and a scientific object, the fact that a scientific object is constructed in the way Wallner indicates does not in itself determine whether there must be one and only one ideally admissible interpretation of it. Further, if, indirectly, interpretations were taken to be not "about" his scientific objects but about something beyond them, that is, at least indirectly about environment, neither singularism nor multiplism are mandated there either. Wallner's notion of environment remains undifferentiated, without the identity conditions required of objects of interpretation for them to answer to either singularism or multiplism. For Wallner, differentiation comes only with the constitution of scientific objects.

Also notice that Wallner's situating reality in the domain of cognitive worlds, understood as "the result of construction," in itself makes no commitment as to whether there is an alternativity of admissible constructions. His constructive realism is distinct from the claim of alternativity, although the latter is compatible with the former. So Wallner's constructive realism joins Harré's and Harrison and Hanna's constructive realism in so far as they entail neither singularism nor multiplism. And with respect to an undifferentiated environment, neither singularism nor multiplism apply.

Let us now add to our inventory of constructive realists and see if corresponding points hold good for the ontology of Hilary Putnam and his associate, Chhanda Gupta.

NOTES

1. Bernard Harrison and Patricia Hanna, *Word and World: Reference and Linguistic Convention,* abbreviated as *"W and W."* Page references are to the unpublished manuscript.

2. Harrison and Hanna, *W and W,* 33.

3. Harrison and Hanna, *W and W,* 33–34.

4. Harrison and Hanna, *W and W,* 35.

5. Harrison and Hanna, *W and W,* 35.

6. Harrison and Hanna, *W and W,* 37–38.

7. Harrison and Hanna, *W and W,* 42.

8. Harrison and Hanna, *W and W,* 42.

9. Harrison and Hanna, *W and W,* 43.

10. Harrison and Hanna, *W and W,* 8–9.

11. Bernard Harrison, personal communication, October, 19, 1999.

12. Fritz G. Wallner, *How to Deal with Science if You Care for Other Cultures: Constructive Realism in the Intercultural World* (Vienna: Wilhelm Braumüller, 1997), abbreviated as *"HDS."* See also Fritz Wallner, *Constructive Realism: Aspects of a New Epistemological Movement* (Vienna: Braumüller, 1994).

13. Wallner, *HDS,* 50.

14. Wallner, *HDS,* 37–38.

15. Wallner, *HDS,* 39.

16. Wallner, *HDS,* 38.

17. Wallner, *HDS,* 40.

18. Wallner, *HDS,* 38.

19. Wallner, *HDS,* 38.

20. Wallner, *HDS,* 47.

21. Wallner, *HDS,* 38.

22. Wallner, *HDS,* 46.

23. Wallner, *HDS,* 39.

24. Wallner, *HDS,* 39.

25. Wallner, *HDS,* 46.

26. Wallner, *HDS,* 49–50.

27. Wallner, *HDS,* 47.

Chapter Eight

Constructive Realists (III): Putnam and Gupta

PUTNAM'S "INTERNAL REALISM"

Hilary Putnam contrasts his so-called internal realism with "metaphysical realism" that holds that "the world consists of some fixed totality of mind-independent objects. There is exactly one true and complete description of 'the way the world is.'"[1] He adds that metaphysical realism's "favorite point of view is a God's eye point of view."[2] In contrast, Putnam favors the *internalist* perspective, according to which the question

> *what objects does the world consist of?* is a question that it only makes sense to ask *within* a theory or description. Many 'internalist' philosophers, though not all, hold further that there is more than one 'true' theory or description of the world.[3]

Putnam notices that the internalist perspective does not mandate the view (though internalists may also hold) that there is more than one "true" theory or description of the world. That is because internal realism is also compatible with the view that there is only one "true" theory or description of the world.

One central feature of internal realism concerns the very notion of objects and the relation between objects and signs. Putnam says:

> In an internalist view . . . signs do not intrinsically correspond to objects, independently of how those signs are employed and by whom. But a sign that is actually employed in a particular way by a particular community of users can correspond to particular objects *within the conceptual scheme of those users.* "Objects" do not exist independently of conceptual schemes. We cut up the world into objects when we introduce one or another scheme of description.

Since the objects *and* the signs are alike *internal* to the scheme of description, it is possible to say what matches what.[4]

Putnam explicates his internalist view by way of comparison with that of Kant when he says that Kant

> does not doubt that there is *some* mind-independent reality; for him this is virtually a postulate of reason. He refers to the element of this mind-independent reality in various terms: thing-in-itself (*Ding an sich*); the noumenal objects or *noumena,* collectively, *the noumenal world.* But we can form no real conception of these noumenal things; even the notion of a noumenal world is a kind of limit of thought (*Grenz-Begriff*) rather than a clear concept.[5]

But Kant's talk of noumenal *objects* notwithstanding, there are no denumerable noumenal objects that correspond to phenomenal objects. And that, according to Putnam, is why Kant must forswear a correspondence theory of truth. Putnam says:

> On Kant's view, any judgment about external or internal objects (physical things or mental entities) says that the noumenal world *as a whole* [emphasis added] is such that this is the description that a rational being (one with our rational nature) given the information available to a being with our sense organs (a being with our sensible nature) would *construct* [emphasis added]. In *that* sense, the judgment ascribes a Power. But the Power is ascribed *to the whole noumenal world;* you must not think that because there are chairs and horses and sensations in our representation, that there are correspondingly noumenal chairs and noumenal horses and noumenal sensations. *There is not even a one-to-one correspondence between things-for-us and things in themselves.*[6]

Individuated objects do not appear at the noumenal level. So individuated objects do not *come as individuated* from the noumenal realm.

No supposedly noumenal "objects" are countable. Countability is not a property of that which is external to a system of counting. So at that level the issue of singularism versus multiplism does not arise. What matters is not so much that there is or is not such a noumenal order. What does matter is that even if there were such an order it could not contain countable objects, objects that would allow one to talk coherently about there being a *common* object between conflicting interpretations. *The condition of commonality of objects of interpretation addressed by otherwise contesting interpretations would fail.* And with that failure, the interpretive ideals of singularism and multiplism could not apply to a whole noumenal order, whether real or not. Under these conditions neither singularism nor multiplism could apply. Yet singularism or multiplism might still apply after denumerable objecthood had been bestowed within a theory or description.

Kant's idea of a noumenal world helps to sharpen our distinction between internal and external constructive realism. That is, if one were to posit that a whole noumenal world were there—providing the "materia" for the construction of real objects—one would be an external constructive realist. And if, other things being equal, one were to forswear the noumenal world, one would be an internal constructive realist. Given what Putnam says about the construction of *objects* within systems of counting from "experiential inputs" we may count him as an external constructive realist. He says:

> Internalism does not deny that there are experiential *inputs* to knowledge; knowledge is not a story with no constraints except *internal* coherence; but it does deny that there are any inputs *which are not themselves to some extent shaped by our concepts,* by the vocabulary we use to report and describe them, or any inputs *which admit of only one description, independent of all conceptual choices.* . . . The very inputs upon which our knowledge is based are conceptually contaminated inputs; but contaminated inputs are better than none.[7]

The external constructive realist holds that some presystematic materia needs to be appealed to in order to account for the construction of real existing objects. While Putnam denies that "there are any inputs which are not themselves to some extent shaped by our concepts," and while he affirms that they are "conceptually contaminated," his view allows the minimal claim that there is presystematic materia "upon which our knowledge is based." This is enough to qualify him as an external constructive realist.

But whether or not we count Putnam as an internal or an external constructive realist, it remains that his would-be inputs are not countable independent of internalist considerations of individuation. And that is what is necessary for the applicability of singularist or multiplist conditions.

CONCEPTUAL RELATIVISM

Putnam's internal realism rejects the notion of an intrinsic property, "a property something has 'in itself,' apart from any contribution made by language or the mind."[8] In contrast, all things and their features should be understood in relational terms as expressed in his idea of *conceptual relativism*.

And Putnam takes internal realism to be compatible with his conceptual relativism. He says:

> Internal realism is, at bottom, just the insistence that realism is *not* incompatible with conceptual relativity. One can be *both* a realist *and* a conceptual relativist. Realism (with a small 'r') has already been introduced: as was said, it is a view

that takes our familiar commonsense scheme, as well as our scientific and artistic and other schemes, at face value, without helping itself to the notion of the thing 'in itself.' But what is conceptual relativity?[9]

By way of explicating conceptual relativism Putnam provides a now famous mereological example. He says:

> We can identify 'individual,' 'object,' 'particular,' etc., and find no absurdity in a world with just three objects which are independent, unrelated 'logical atoms.' But there are perfectly good logical doctrines which lead to different results.
>
> Suppose, for example, that like some Polish logicians, I believe that for every two particulars there is an object which is their sum. (This is the basic assumption of 'mereology,' the calculus of parts and wholes invented by Lezniewski.) If I ignore, for the moment, the so-called 'null object,' then I find that the world of 'three individuals' (as Carnap might have had it, at least when he was doing inductive logic) actually contains **seven** objects.
>
> Now, the classic metaphysical realist way of dealing with such problems is well-known. It is to say that there is a single world (think of this as a piece of dough) which we can slice into pieces in different ways. But this 'cookie cutter' metaphor founders on the question, 'What are the "parts" of this dough?' If the answer is that **O, x1, x2, x3, x1+x2, x1+x3, x2+x3, x1+x2+x3** are all the different 'pieces', then we have not a *neutral* description, but rather a *partisan* description—just the description of the Warsaw logician! And it is no accident that metaphysical realism cannot really recognize the phenomenon of conceptual relativity—for that phenomenon turns on the fact that *the logical primitives themselves, and in particular the notions of object and existence, have a multitude of different uses rather than one absolute 'meaning.'*[10]

On Putnam's account, there is no nonpartisan way of identifying pertinent objects and their existence. Thus, one cannot establish the would-be commonality of the external objects required by otherwise contending conceptual schemes. While there may indeed be contending interpretations of objects *within* a given conceptual scheme, and while there may be one or more admissible interpretations within that scheme, where (as in the mereological case) there are differing conceptual schemes, different "worlds" of objects would obtain. And so what might otherwise look like contending schemes over the same external objects would turn out not to be so. If no external objects can be fixed as common, pertinent schemes cannot compete over them. At that level, neither singularism nor multiplism could obtain. If we cannot ask whether the object is one and the same as between systems of counting, then the ideals of singularism or multiplism cannot apply as between such systems.

Putnam's philosophy holds that realism is compatible with the alternativity of conceptual schemes. But the alternativity of conceptual schemes does not entail multiplism, for, according to Putnam, the very question whether the objects spoken *of* by the alternative conceptual schemes are the same objects cannot arise. That is, while there may be one or more admissible interpretations of an object within a given conceptual scheme, the question of whether there are one or more admissible interpretations of an object beyond those schemes makes no sense. Putnam's internal realism with its rider of conceptual relativism (or alternativity) entails neither singularism nor multiplism.

CONTRA PROJECTION

We should take heed of Putnam's warning that the claim that things and their properties should be understood in relational terms should not itself be taken to imply that one can *project* or *impute* properties where, by thinking of or willing something in a certain way, it takes on those properties. Putnam's kind of constructivism does not amount to a projectivism or an imputationism. Putnam expresses his concern this way.

> Projection is thinking of something as having properties it does not have, but that we can imagine (perhaps because something else we are acquainted with really does have them), without being conscious that this is what we are doing. It is thus a species of *thought*—thought about something.[11]

Putnam distinguishes between projections on the one hand from the relationality of things and their features on the other hand. He holds that things and their features are not projections. While they constitute facts of the matter in relation to conceptual schemes, they are not added to or *projected* or *imputed* by our will. As Chhanda Gupta emphasizes:

> The fact of the matter is that the object which the sentence talks about, itself has the properties it appears to have from a perspective under certain specific conditions. The properties are real, and not mere projections.[12]

Putnam says further:

> 'How many objects are there?' has an answer, namely three in the case of the first version (Carnap's World) and 'seven' (or 'eight') in the case of the second version ('The Polish Logician's World'). Once we make clear how we are using 'object' (or 'exist'), the question 'How many objects exist?' has an answer that is not at all a matter of 'convention.'[13]

While it is a matter of convention which system of counting is deployed, it is not a matter of convention which truths are thus mandated. While one might choose a system of counting, once chosen the truths that result within the system are not a matter of choice. Putnam says:

> Our concepts may be culturally relative, but it does not follow that the truth or falsity of everything we say using those concepts is simply 'decided' by the

culture. But the idea that there is an Archimedean point, or a use of 'exist' inherent in the world itself, from which the question 'How many objects really exist?' makes sense, is an illusion.[14]

Notice that it is not only *objects* that are scheme-relative, according to Putnam. *Existence* is, too. In this regard recall Putnam's assertion that ***"the logical primitives themselves, and in particular the notions of object and existence, have a multitude of different uses rather than one absolute 'meaning.'"***[15] That means that, whatever else one could say about Kant's whole noumenal world, according to Putnam, it cannot be claimed to *exist.*

This point allows us to distinguish transcendental realism from external constructive realism. The transcendental realist takes objects and their features to be real and system-independent. The external constructive realist takes objects and their features to be real and system-dependent, but allows that there is *materia* from which real objects are constructed in pertinent systems.[16]

ON THE CONVENTIONALITY OF COUNTING

One might hold that one system of counting is better than another. For example, one might hold that Carnap's system of counting is better than the Polish system because the Polish system depends upon Carnap's, and not vice versa. That is, the mereological example is generated by positing that there are three (or four) "logical atoms" (a la Carnap) before one can generate further objects by combining them. But even if this were the case, that is not sufficient to establish metaphysical realism. The supposed superiority of the first system over the other does not show that the objects mentioned in the first system are the *really* real objects independent of systems of counting. There is nothing in the conceptual relativist view that suggests that, because systems of counting or conceptual schemes are a matter of choice, there can be no good reasons for such choices. The same point can be seen in a parallel case of two constructed conventions: polygamy and monogamy. To say that they are chosen conventions is not to say that they are *equally* preferable in certain ways of life. From the fact that they are conventions it does not follow that one might not have good reasons for opting for monogamy, for example, in light of certain other views about emotions as experienced and understood in certain cultural circumstances. In turn, one might hold that, with respect to other interests and values, polygamy might be the better convention. In short, one might have an informed discussion about which conventions should be chosen. Conventionality or constructivism does not entail arbitrariness. And nonarbitrariness does not entail metaphysical realism.

GUPTA ON PUTNAM

Fuller implications of internal realism and conceptual relativism may be seen in the contribution of Chhanda Gupta. In her lucid book, *Realism versus Realism*, Gupta ramifies Putnam's view by first comparing it to metaphysical realism. She says, first:

> Old-style realism takes a transcendent metaphysical stance, focusing on reality, on what there is in itself independently of what we know or say about it.
>
> Opposed to this are 'realisms' that take an *immanent* stance insisting on the need of linking the question: 'what there is?' with the question: 'what do we conceive, know and say about it?'
>
> A few points may be noted to make the contrast between these two views leap to vision. They also highlight the main strands of the type of realism I have tried to defend following Putnam's lead.[17]

In a series of paired statements Gupta contrasts transcendental realism with immanent or internal realism. I shall comment on each pair in turn. Gupta says:

> 1. Things exist independently and must be described too in terms that have nothing to do with us, according to transcendental realists. Things have features intrinsically, non-relationally, and not as objects of anyone's belief, thought, experience and knowledge. This is the requirement of absoluteness.
>
> 1'. Things and their features do exist independently and are not our own making, the internal realists maintain like all realists. These are not projections and reifications of our own conceptual and cognitive nature, and are in this sense nonepistemic. But internal realism maintains additionally that such realities can be intelligibly talked about only when construed as thinkable, knowable and describable. No meaningful discourse is possible about anything, including its most fundamental features, unless it is an object, at least a putative object of some belief, conception or knowledge. To stress the relativity of things and their features to thought in this way however, is not to deny that things exist whether or not we know or say anything about them. Relativity here means that things which we may or may not know are not transcendent, that is, they are not trans-conceptual, trans-cognitive and trans-phenomenal.[18]

Consider the requirement of "absoluteness" (in 1) propounded by the transcendent realist, namely that "things have features intrinsically, non-relationally, and not as objects of anyone's belief, thought, experience and knowledge." First, intrinsicality, nonrelationality, and independence of beliefs, thought, experience, and knowledge entail neither singularism nor multiplism. That is, each of the conditions of the requirement of absoluteness is compatible with one or more ideally admissible interpretations. From the absolute independence of epistemic activity, it does not follow that one or more than one interpretation would be admissible. Transcendental realism is detachable from singularism and multiplism.

Second, the independence of beliefs, thoughts, experience, and knowledge could be construed in either individualist or social terms. Gupta puts the point in individual terms. She could also have put the point in social terms. The epistemic conditions construed socially would show themselves in such collective conditions as practices, norms, and the like. Accordingly, Gupta's denial of the possibility of "projections" disallows the sort of route taken by individual as well as social projectivists or imputationists. Accordingly, things and their features, as she says, are "not projections and reifications of our own conceptual and cognitive nature, and are in this sense nonepistemic."

Third, Gupta's characterization of transcendental realism suggests that it endorses the thought that things "must be *described* [my emphasis] . . . in terms that have nothing to do with us." This way of characterizing transcendental realism immediately makes the view suspect, for description as such has everything to do with us. Yet a transcendental realist could drop this requirement.

Consider now Gupta's characterization of the favored internal realist position (1'). Notice what differentiates transcendental realism from internal realism. It concerns what "can be intelligibly talked about," namely that which is "construed as thinkable, knowable and describable." Accordingly, for the internal realist, "No meaningful discourse is possible about anything . . . unless it is an object, at least a putative object of some belief, conception or knowledge." This leaves it open "that things exist whether or not we know or say anything about them." That is how it is both that things which we may or may not know "are not trans-conceptual, trans-cognitive and trans-phenomenal" and at the same time are not (individual or social) projections. Gupta's contrast continues further when she says:

> 2. Things and their features according to transcendental realists are *radically nonepistemic* in the sense of being entirely independent of *all* beliefs and conceptions. This is another way of saying that all our beliefs and conceptions may remain just as they are and yet reality and truth about reality may be entirely different from what we believe and conceive.
>
> 2'. Things and their features according to internal realists on the contrary are *nonepistemic simpliciter,* not radically nonepistemic. They are so in the sense that they are not of our own making. The features are real, not projected on to something which does not have them. Nevertheless they are what we conceive and believe them to be (in numerous cases).[19]

Gupta characterizes transcendental realism as holding that "things and their features . . . are *radically nonepistemic* in the sense of their being entirely independent of *all* beliefs and conceptions." According to Gupta's account of transcendental realism, things and their features are entirely independent of all beliefs and conceptions. Gupta explicates the point by saying that "reality and truth about reality may be entirely different from what we believe and conceive." In contrast, she suggests that internal realists are not *radically* nonepistemic. Yet things and their features, on her account, "are what we conceive them to be (in numerous cases)." We get a clue as to how this might be so in (3'). Gupta says:

3. Transcendental realism perpetuates the reality/appearance divide.

3'. Internal realism rejects the dichotomy. The way things appear are the way they really are.[20]

And Gupta's contrast continues still further when she says:

4. Transcendental realists regard the world in itself and things that have intrinsic features by themselves as real. This tempts one to label appearances as unreal. There is no knowing, according to them, whether what appears is really what a thing is by itself. This suits the skeptic's game plan.

4'. Internal realists believe that things really do have the features, even the most fundamental features, which our best available theories conceive and believe them to have.[21]

According to (4'), "things really do have the features . . . which our best available theories conceive and believe them to have." How is this possible? It is so because, going back to (1'), an object must be thought to be an "object of some belief, conception or knowledge." That is, the very condition of intelligibility is built into the notion of an object (or reality, or any cognate thereof). So the reality and objectivity of things is internal to the notion of a real object; hence *internal* realism. So understood, the very idea of the transcendental realist who holds that reality might be radically different from how we conceive it to be is incoherent.

In sum, the dual claim of internal realism is that (a) a real thing and its features are independent of anyone's belief, thought, experience, and knowledge. They are not of anyone's making. (Constructivists deny this.) At the same time, (b) the condition of intelligibility is built into the notion of an object (or reality) such that it is "thinkable, knowable and describable." Accordingly, while no particular properties or features of a thing are projectable or imputable onto that thing (that is, no object takes on or gets properties added to it), it remains that objects and their features are "thinkable, knowable and describable." The first is a condition of *independence*, and the second is a condition of *intelligibility*.

For our overriding purposes the critical point is that the internal realist's conditions of independence and intelligibility are each compatible with either singularism or multiplism. The conditions of independence and intelligibility are each compatible with the claim that there is one and only one ideally admissible interpretation of an object and with the claim that there may be more than one ideally admissible interpretation.

Let us collect our findings. Thom, Harré, and Harrison and Hanna suggest that there is practice-independent "materia" that enter into the constitution of objects of interpretation. In Thom's case it is what he calls the "further object." In Harré's case it is the "world-stuff." In Harrison and Hanna's case it is that which has "the power to deliver a verdict of true or false on judgments formulated in terms of the things and features constructed in terms of given practices." Insofar as they posit *something* beyond interpretive practices—not yet amounting to real objects—they are external constructive realists. As well, while Putnam holds that the question "*what objects does the world consist of?* is a question that it only makes sense to ask *within* a theory or description,"[22] his view allows the minimal claim that there is presystematic "input" or "materia" on the basis of which existing objects are to be constituted. This qualifies Putnam as an external constructive realist.

In any case, neither internal nor external constructive realism entails either singularism or multiplism. Countability arises only at the practice-dependent level, and countability is a necessary condition for the applicability of singularism and multiplism. This point will be emphasized in the next chapter when we consider the internal constructive realism of Joseph Margolis.

NOTES

1. Hilary Putnam, *Reason, Truth, and History* (Cambridge: Cambridge University Press, 1981), 49. Abbreviated as "RTH."

2. Putnam, RTH, 49.

3. Putnam, RTH, 49.

4. Putnam, RTH, 52.

5. Putnam, RTH, 61.

6. Putnam, RTH, 63.

7. Putnam, RTH, 54.

8. Hilary Putnam, *The Many Faces of Realism* (LaSalle, Ill.: Open Court, 1987), 8. Abbreviated as "MFR."

9. Putnam, MFR, 17.

10. Putnam, MFR, 18–19.

11. Putnam, MFR, 11–12.

12. Chhanda Gupta, *Realism versus Realism* (Calcutta: Allied Publishers, 1995), 69. Abbreviated as "RvR."

13. Putnam, MFR, 20.

14. Putnam, MFR, 20.

15. Putnam, MFR, 19.

16. Here English grammar misleads. To identify "materia" as either plural or singular begs the question of its countability. To emphasize the point I use the singular for "materia."

17. Gupta, RvR, ix.
18. Gupta, RvR, ix–x.
19. Gupta, RvR, x.
20. Gupta, RvR, x.
21. Gupta, RvR, x–xi.
22. Putnam, RTH, 49.

Chapter Nine

Constructive Realists (IV): Margolis

The difference between *internal* and *external* constructive realism is that the former appeals to nothing that precedes a symbol system and the latter appeals to some "materia," be it Thom's "further object" or Harré's "world-stuff," Wallner's "environment," or Harrison and Hanna's "that which has the power to deliver a verdict of true or false," and so forth. The external constructive realist holds that, although it cannot be countenanced as embodying *real objects,* some presystematic "materia" needs to be appealed to in order to account for the construction of real objects. In contrast, the internal constructive realist holds that there is nothing *there* or we can make no sense of the claim that there is something *there* outside symbol systems.

Consider now the constructive realism of Joseph Margolis that subtends claims of real existents under a second-order constructivism. His is an internal constructive realism. I shall suggest that a singularist might actually agree with Margolis's internal constructive realism. But he or she would disagree with Margolis's further claim of alternativity, that is, that there is a multiplicity of admissible and incongruent interpretations of cultural objects. So understood, Margolis's rider of alternativity is distinct and detachable from his ontology of internal constructive realism.

In numerous works Margolis embraces the theses of (a) cognitive intransparency, (b) the historicity of thinking, (c) the symbiosis of subject and object, and (d) the social constructionism of the self.[1] Taken together, these theses suggest that there is no first philosophy. They lead to the general conclusion that there is no unique solution to interesting philosophical issues. He embraces

> a strengthened adherence to the cognitive intransparency of the world; an increasingly radicalized sense of the historical nature and conditions of human existence; an insistence on the horizoned, preformed, fragmentary, biased

cognitive and affective orientation of human life; the impossibility of extricating reason, inquiry, the reflexive critique of any judgment or commitment from any of the above conditions; the recognition of divergent and moderately incommensurable conceptual schemes compatible with the survival of the race; the likelihood that our perceptual and critical acquaintance with the world has been and continues to be heavily overdetermined in theorizing and conceptualizing respects; the realization that we cannot in principle distinguish between the constructed nature of our intelligible world and the "independent" structure of the brute world; and the admission of the real-world impossibility of ever judging, except under endogenous constraints, whether we are actually approaching closer to an understanding of all possible conceptual schemes or, using this scheme or that, closer to the fixed Truth about the world.[2]

Margolis holds that cultural entities, including historical events, emerge from a "precultural" domain. Yet the precultural domain, which includes relatively stable referents and is part of the physical natural world, is constituted. While the constituting is not normally subject to change, it has a history. For Margolis the physical is a characterization of things with which humans interact. Since humans do not interact with "brute reality," Margolis does not equate brute reality with the physical. Yet to say that humans constitute the physical is not to say that the physical is constituted in arbitrary ways. As Margolis says:

> We open our eyes and see a world we cannot ignore; still, what we see is due to what we are; and what we are we are as a result of our continuous self-formation and transformation within a larger history and the larger processes of nature. So the 'resistance' of the encountered world is not at all incompatible with its being 'constituted.'[3]

Margolis's historicism involves his rejecting Aristotle's ontic view that the real is necessarily changeless and that whatever changes there are must be embedded in a changeless order. He rejects the corresponding Aristotelian epistemic view that knowledge must be about the changeless. Alternatively, Margolis allies himself with Protagoras, the author of the theory of the flux, or the theory that the world is in constant change and that it has no constant structure. On Margolis's account, Protagoras held that knowledge could be claimed for some kind of grasp of this changing order. Margolis's so-called fluxism is altogether global. That is, all human activity (including the activity of theorizing about objects of parcelled disciplines) is historical and therefore cultural. Correspondingly, Margolis affirms the double doctrine that (a) the world is not constant, that is, it does not have a changeless structure. And (b) knowledge of that changing order (including logic, mathematics, science, morality, interpretation of the arts, or any other similar discipline) is possible.

For Margolis, the notions of sameness and difference are embedded in the interests and uses to which creatures put their intelligence, for there are no invariant or exceptionless, changeless, timeless, universal principles for a thing to properly be a thing of its kind. For him, to use the same predicate does not commit one to an invariant order. One can use the same predicate in a world that is not invariant.

Correspondingly, principles, rules, genres, laws, and the like are abstractions from within some form of life, or practice, or *lebenswelt*, or *lebensform*, or something of that kind. When such forms of life change, the abstractions that arose from earlier enabling cases will have become otiose with respect to new enabling cases and subsequent abstractions. Discourse cannot be formalistically or algorithmically separated from its communicative contexts. At the same time, principles, natural kinds, laws, rules, genres, and other like notions should be reinterpreted in such a way that they save any reasonably well-defined discipline or science. Margolis takes his program—which he calls "an-archic," in contrast with the Aristotelian "archic" project—to be progressive in the sense that it admits of theoretical advance; it allows for a reconstruction of basic ideas such as objectivity, truth, and rationality. According to Margolis's an-archic view, one can recover everything that is needed without losing anything. Accordingly, if one departs from the original archic view it is just not the case that incoherence is inevitable.

One might object that Margolis's theory of the flux is itself subsumable under an "archic" model. For example, Heraclitus's theory of the flux can be seen as a specification of a higher-order arché, itself an ahistorical principle. But this would be to misunderstand how radical Margolis's proposal is. Not only does he embrace the historicity of particular things, persons, interpreters, and objects of their interpretation. He holds further that the very frameworks or conceptual schemes or symbol systems in terms of which persons understand anything at all cannot be presumed to be fixed outside the context of theorizing to start with. This means that no sense can be made of archic principles, whether they be "the permanent" of Parmenides, or "the flux" of Heraclitus. Heraclitus is still too conservative for Margolis, and it is with this thought that Margolis seeks to reinstate his patron saint Protagoras, who was so dismissed by his contemporaries and ignored by ours. It was he who deeply threatened the archic tradition of his own time.

Further, according to Margolis's an-archic view, the cognizing subject and the cognized world are symbiotically related. Thus Margolis moves neither from reality to knowledge (or from ontology to epistemology) as the ancients did, nor from knowledge to reality, as the idealists did. In the first case, Margolis remarks that Aristotle does not tell us why we should suppose that the structure of the real world should be given priority over what it is we claim to know. Further, he notes that Kant's bifurcation of subject and object—which effectively denies the unanalyzability of the subject–object symbiosis—is precisely what makes it possible for Kant to theorize that there are *invariant* concepts of understanding in terms of which the world is understood. Rather, on Margolis's view we postulate both the cognizing agent and the cognized world within a space of "critical reflection," as he puts it. They cannot be disjoined in the way that Kant attempts. The concepts under which we understand the world are themselves historical and changeable. Correspondingly, the knowing subject has no fixed structure but is a center of cognitive activity that is open to change over time.

This view suggests the idea that human beings are social constructions and cannot be supposed to have invariant structures of understanding. Such a social constructionism runs counter to Kant's and Husserl's projects that, according to Margolis, pursued the epistemological counterpart of what Aristotle was doing in ontology. Namely, for them, at the end of inquiry there is a fixed set of concepts in terms of which our world is rendered intelligible. That account fails to come to terms with the fact that the concepts we use are used under certain conditions of historical preformation. Margolis holds that we cannot exit from this condition in order to claim to be moving in the direction of a unitary account of the changeless conditions of understanding. Correspondingly, human beings have no essential or fixed natures. Rather, they transform or make themselves.

Margolis says that the symbiosis of subject and object (or of word and world, or of the cognizing and cognized) is, in a special sense, a *myth.* It is a conceptual posit. It provides the space in which distributive claims can be made. Put otherwise, such myths provide the "context of all contexts," or the context in which all distributive claims can be made. Consequently, the thought that subject and object are symbiotically related cannot itself be a distributive truth-claim, because distributive truth-claims are posited within the space such a myth provides. On this account, the very distinction between epistemology and ontology depends upon our being situated in relation to an organizing myth. This distinction is not given independently of a theoretical context, and it may be construed in different ways, depending upon various mythic contexts.

Since one is never in a privileged position independent of the context of all contexts, the claim of realism can be made only internally. Such a realism allows for such claims as that certain scientific theories enable us to intervene in nature. However, to say that realism is internal rather than external to a subject–object symbiosis does not prohibit us from saying many of the same things about particular things that the naive or direct realist wants to say. On his account, the an-archic view admits the range of distributive claims one might wish to make in an archic scheme and more, except, of course, for the modal claim of the flux that the archic scheme denies. While the an-archic view allows that our survival depends upon our contact with a real world, the specific details of that world are always a construction under the conditions of history. Further, this internal realism is not tantamount to idealism, for idealism denies the unanalyzable symbiosis between subject and object.

This sort of constructive realism does not inhibit one from distinguishing the reality of the cultural world from the reality of the physical world. In the cultural world, as opposed to the physical world, humans are both the subject and the object of discourse. They are trying to understand *themselves*. This is a remark about a difference in the direction of respective inquiries, and not about the natures of things independent of pertinent practices. Correspondingly, objectivity, neutrality, and cognate notions may be unpacked differently by the human sciences and by the physical sciences. The kind of neutrality that may obtain in the physical sciences may not obtain in the human sciences. Unpacking such notions on either side should be understood to be internal to the assumed subject–object symbiosis. As Margolis says:

> *what counts as objectivity is—ineluctably—a reasoned artifact of how we choose to discipline our truth-claims in any sector of inquiry.* The assumption is that there is simply no way to discover the true norms of objectivity in any domain at all. Acceptable norms will have to be constructed as one or another disputed second-order proposal fitted to what we claim our best interests are in this domain or that.[4]

Again, Margolis holds that all distributive claims are contexted. And distributive discourse cannot provide its own discursive context. Yet we develop pictures of the inclusive context within which our distributive discourse proceeds. At the same time, we cannot make truth-claims about such pictures. We cannot distributively talk about the context of discourse, for doing so would violate the conditions under which we could distributively talk in the first place. In this way there is a permanent limit to the inclusiveness of our distributive discourse. We cannot escape this mythic dimension. The mythic is not determinately there beyond the discursive. Rather, the mythic is embedded at every point in the discourse in which we speak. Every discursive utterance implicates the inclusive universe of discourse in which it and every other such utterance belongs. We can speak of myths. Yet, the "context of all contexts" cannot itself be a determinate referent of distributive truth-valued discourse. We implicate it, but we can never invoke it so as to make it the subject of some further remark.

Put otherwise, on Margolis's account all distributive claims have truth-value (or are truth-valued like), but pertinent myths do not; they are neither true nor false, nor are they subject to evidence or argumentation of the sort characteristically offered in support of distributive claims. Part of the reason for this is that, if all discourses are contexted, one cannot come to the limit of the space in which the truth-claims are made. And so it is impossible to speak about such discourse *as such* in terms that resemble how we speak about claims within a discourse. On Margolis's view, the mythic, as context for discursive claims, is not "foregrounded" for justification in the ways that discursive claims characteristically are. Being backgrounded, it remains unfathomed at any particular moment in the emergence of inquiry. We cannot speak about discourse from the outside, for any apparently successful attempt to do so will but expand the discourse and so we will have failed to speak from its "outside." But we are not left dumb at this stage, for there are ways of speaking about myths or the context of all contexts that are not truth-valued.

Margolis's thesis of the symbiosis between subject and object precludes a piecemeal approach at the second order. The piecemeal approach could be adopted only on the condition that there are some domains whose objects answer to a nonsymbiotized realist construal, say, and other domains whose objects answer to a nonsymbiotized constructivist construal. But Margolis asserts that nonsymbiotized realism or constructivism cannot be defended. Rather realism and constructivism are symbiotically related in such a way that the real is constructed and the constructed is real. The symbiotized relation between subject and object is a general condition that obtains quite irrespective of particular objects or domains of concern. So, for Margolis there is no way of articulating a piecemeal ontology. Still, within the context of the symbiosis one can distinguish cultural discourses from natural discourses from mathematical discourses, and so on. Specifically, Margolis distinguishes the cultural from the natural by observing that cultural entities characteristically have intentional structures while natural entities do not. Denying the globalism of the theory of the flux would (contrary to Margolis) be tantamount to affirming that the cognizing self and the cognized world are not symbiotized in some universe of discourse and that such universes are not artifactually posited. On Margolis's view, one gives up the idea of *de re* necessities: there are no necessary structures in the world. *Yet this allows apparent necessities, seen as such from within the perspective of one's historical place. Whatever necessities obtain are apparent and internal to a discourse that itself is not necessary.* Whatever regularities appear in the ongoing inquiry of a society are, in this way, posited. Only *de re* necessity is denied. Specifically in the case of mathematics, Margolis holds that one manipulates uninterpreted formal systems and posited entities, assuming certain axioms, postulates, rule of derivation, and the like. They are comprised by completely artifactual games. Correspondingly, mathematical entities are nominalizations of mathematical predicables. Claims about the reality of such entities are made within the context of a symbiotized language that is posited in a historical circumstance. While one may say that numbers are real, that cannot be taken to mean that they exist outside the horizon of one's state of inquiry at a particular historically constituted moment.[5]

In sum, no viable constructivism cannot but be realist, and no viable realism cannot but be constructivist. As Margolis says:

constructivism is *not* (or need not be) an abandonment of realism. Rather, I believe, there can be no viable realisms that are not also constructivisms; no other strategy . . . can escape incoherence and unacceptable paradox. This is as true of the natural world as it is of the cultural.[6]

One consideration Margolis adduces for his constructive realism concerns the case of language, which for him exemplifies cultural achievements quite generally. If one allows that natural languages are real and that they are not independent of interpretive activities, then the very notions of realism and constructivism cannot be allowed mutual exclusivity. As Margolis says:

> it does not make sense to claim that natural languages are *real* in any way that is said to be entirely independent of the discursive and interpretive activities of a society of apt speakers. Natural languages are real "in spite of" any such dependence. . . . But if languages are real if spoken (or written) by apt speakers, then, plainly, *any* realism that claimed unconditionally that whatever *is* real *is* "fully constituted, autonomous and independent of any interpretive activity" must mean at least that language and artworks are not real at all![7]

The constructivist's idea of the real is not robust enough. The realist's idea goes too far. For whatever is taken as the real, on Margolis's account, cannot escape the fact that any claim of the real must be subtended under the matrix of "historied" human practices. For Margolis, any claim of the real is subtended under a second-order constructivism. He emphasizes the point when he says:

> there can be no viable realism that is not also a constructivism; because, of course, the cultural world comprises entities that are culturally constituted, and because we ourselves are similarly constituted by the enculturing powers of an existing society of selves . . . it's perfectly all right to treat the physical world as independent of human inquiry and interpretation; but it is *not* possible to make sense of doing so without conceding that it—and every would-be determinate truth *about that world*—is epistemically constructed in accord with our cognitive abilities.[8]

Recall our distinction between internal and external constructive realism. The view that there is nothing or nothing intelligible that is not constructed in accord with our cognitive capacities is an *internal* constructive realism. In contrast, the view that there is something that is not so constructed is an *external* constructive realism. Margolis's view is the former.

Accordingly, Margolis summarizes his internal constructive realism this way.

> The only coherent theory of the independence of the real world admits: *(a)* that the *ontic* independence of the natural world is a posit of our *epistemic* constructions—noumena need not apply; *(b)* that the world of human culture is, therefore, as much entitled to realist standing, though it cannot be independent in the sense of *(a)*; *(c)* that the realist standing of the natural world entails and presup-

poses the realist standing of the cultural world, particularly the standing of
selves or persons (ourselves); and *(d)* that ontic and epistemic questions are inherently inseparable, or meaningless if separated, though they are not the same.[9]

Margolis emphasizes the cultural artifactuality of the physical world and
knowledge generally when he says that:

> although we conjecture (reasonably, of course) that the physical world is older
> than the advent of human culture, the conjecture itself occurs only within the
> space of the human: knowledge is a cultural artifact; also, the determinate struc-
> tures we impute to the physical world (what we take realism to signify) are . . .
> logically inseparable from the emergent powers of the human world. In short,
> our theories of the physical world are endogenously horizoned by the cognitive
> history of human science.[10]

And again:

> the confirmation of any claim (whether first- or second-order) cannot but be
> *lebensformlich* and historicized—ultimately consensual but not criterial. To
> admit all that is to admit that ontic and epistemic and interpreted fixities are ar-
> tifacts of our contingent practices.[11]

Notice that the claim that there is no principled distinction between realism
and constructivism does not entail that for a given object of interpretation
there is one or more than one ideally admissible interpretation of it. Yet if
such a constructive realism is neutral with respect to singularism or multiplism, that need not mean that no broadly metaphysical considerations pertain
to the objectivity of judgments concerning the range of ideally admissible interpretations. For Margolis the grounds for such objectivity are to be found in
the Intentionality (in his special sense) of cultural objects. And Intentionality
allows for either singularism or multiplism. Margolis emphasizes the place of
Intentionality in interpretive matters when he says:

> Many who offer theories of interpretation . . . confidently affirm (without suc-
> cess) that they avoid all metaphysical entanglements. They cannot be right . . .
> we cannot claim to be neutral, there, *if* we also mean to secure interpretation's
> objectivity. For, of course, if interpretive objectivity *depends* on the nature of In-
> tentional properties and on whether they *are* significantly different from the non-
> Intentional physical properties of natural things, then the disclaimer will count
> for very little.[12]

Yet we *can* agree that Intentionality bears on objectivity and still affirm that
whether one is a realist or a constructivist or a constructive realist does not
entail either singularism or multiplism. To suggest that ontology in the narrow sense is detachable from ideality does not disallow—as Margolis thinks
it does—that other "metaphysical" issues are ruled out of court.

The question whether Intentionality mandates singularism or multiplism involves explicating the idea of (a) Intentional properties, (b) number and nature, and (c) the identity of cultural entities. I shall comment on each in turn.

(a) Here are several formulations of Intentional properties that Margolis offers.

> Intentional predicables . . . differ from other predicables in being inherently interpretable. They are inherently significative, semiotic linguistic, representational, expressive, historical. They are *determinable* for that reason in a potentially puzzling way: they are made determinate by way of interpretation and they remain interpretively determinable by further alternative interpretations. They are *not* simply indeterminate; and artworks possessing such properties are not thereby rendered inherently "incomplete"—as the phenomenologists are fond of saying: Roman Ingarden for instance.[13]

Notice that Margolis defines Intentional properties in terms of their *determinability*, the latter condition not amounting to incompleteness. Such properties remain interpretively determinable by further interpretive activity. And Margolis further outlines his special notion of Intentionality in this way.

> *Intentional* properties [mean] (a) that they designate meanings assignable to certain structures or meaningful structures, (b) as a result of the various forms of culturally informed activity (speech, deeds, manufacture, artistic creation), such that (c) suitably informed persons may claim to discern such properties and interpret them objectively. "Intentionality" is a term of art here, which I designate by capitalizing the initial "I." I use it predicatively, to mark a family of *sui generis* properties confined to the cultural world: that is, to designate the collective, intrinsically interpretable features of societal life, *not* (therefore) equivalent to the essentially solipsistic, ahistorical, and acultural forms of intentionality featured in the theories of Brentano and Husserl.[14]

Margolis goes on to tie Intentional properties to consensuality. As he says:

> The pivot of the argument has never been more than this: that cultural phenomena must have realist standing; that admitting that is admitting the metaphysical peculiarities of Intentional properties . . . I mean that our cognitive practices are broadly consensual, competent without being grounded in foundational propositions or fixed criteria. The argument applies in the natural sciences as well as in the interpretation of art and history.[15]

Granting the consensuality and informality of Intentional properties, multiplism is still not mandated. A singularist might allow both determinability as well as consensuality. That is, the idea that cognitive practices are broadly consensual commits one to neither singularism nor multiplism, for consensuality might eventuate in closure to a limit of one, or it might not. The issue of consensuality is distinct from the issue of ideality.

(b) Margolis closely ties the idea of Intentionality to that of *nature* in contrast to *number*. He says:

> there is a run of phenomena—events and particulars—that "have natures" that intrinsically include complex *intentional* properties, such that those natures or features are vague or indeterminate enough to invite incongruent judgments regarding what they are, or such that their natures and properties are so alterable by interpretation alone that incongruent judgments cannot be avoided in specifying them. The principal site of such phenomena is, of course, the world of human culture—artworks, actions, histories, and the psychological nature of persons, institutions, theories, practices, and whatever is similarly affected when colored by cultural interests.[16]

I have already indicated that the indeterminacy of objects of interpretation need not on that account "invite incongruent judgments." A singularist might urge that a singularist condition might indeed obtain where the indeterminacy of an interpretation "matches" the indeterminacy of the object in question. Or one might urge that, because of the indeterminacy in question one should remain silent about whether singularism or multiplism obtains. The point is that multiplism is not entailed by the indeterminacy of pertinent objects.

Margolis presses his case by restricting determinability to the nature and not the number of an object of interpretation. According to Margolis's usage, number pertains to reference and nature pertains to predication. So understood, alterability by interpretation (or imputation) concerns predication (nature) and not reference (or number). He says:

> The formal distinction between reference and predication affords no epistemic license for believing that the interpretation of cultural entities (no matter how labile) affects in any way the "number" or self-identity of the real entities that are being interpreted.[17]

Once Margolis distinguishes between nature and number, how are we to understand an entity's condition of identity or individuation? Margolis answers:

> I recommend . . . that we treat "entity" in a very lax way: allowing, as an "entity," anything that we are prepared to say exists as an individuated *denotatum,* about which predicative claims can be made and validated.[18]

Again, according to Margolis's distinctive usage, cultural entities are indeterminate but determinable as regards their nature, allowing that natures may be transfigured in the course of their careers. As he says:

> artworks and other cultural entities *are not indeterminate* at all. They are, rather, numerically *determinate* in the same sense physical objects are and predicatively *determinable sui generis.*[19]

Margolis holds fairly fixed the entity's identity while allowing that its nature may change. I say fairly fixed, for we should keep in mind Margolis's underlying fluxist notion (already rehearsed) that there are no principled necessities, only contingent ones.

(c) We now face perhaps the central challenge of Margolis's effort, namely, how to reconcile the identity of cultural entities with their determinability. That is, can the thesis be sustained that, with the determinability of Intentional properties of a cultural entity, it remains one and the same entity throughout its transformation? If no satisfactory case can be made that the entity remains one and the same over time, then, "it" cannot answer to competing interpretations. Without such a case, Margolis's general "robust relativist" project collapses.

Margolis affirms that the self-identity (as to number) of a cultural entity is not determinable. Its identity conditions are not alterable by imputation. He says:

> the self-identity of a history (Collingwood's example) or of an artwork (or of a stone, for that matter) cannot be said, coherently, to be altered merely as a result of particular predications. I insist on the point, because many critics of relativism suppose that the relativist *shifts the identity of what interpretation addresses* in order to make out a plausible case.[20]

He ramifies the point in this way:

> although the interpretation of a history or artwork or sentence cannot, for reasons of conceptual coherence, alter the identity of any *denotatum,* the interpretation of Intentionally qualified entries can indeed alter the "nature" of what may be thereafter interpreted. . . . All we require is a careful distinction between the predicative oddities of artworks and their denotative fixity.[21]

But, finally, can Margolis sustain a principled distinction between "predicative oddities" and their denotative fixity? I suggest that the principled distinction that Margolis requires to distinguish number from nature is undercut by his own pan-fluxism, for the thesis of the flux puts into doubt any denotative fixity of pertinent entities. The same issue arises in another way. When speaking of Intentional objects Margolis speaks of interpretive determin*ability,* by which he means determinability as to nature. Margolis says:

> artworks . . . are *not fully determinate but are, characteristically, interpretively determinable* in Intentional ways . . . in spite of having such a nature, they are reasonably *determinate in number,* individuable, and reidentifiable.[22]

The thought is that, holding the numerical identity of an artwork relatively fixed, its nature is variously determinable. So the nature of cultural achievements can be made more determinate by culturally informed activity. As a result, one can then discover those works as having the properties ascribed to them. Margolis's imputationist thesis applies to the nature of numerically distinct artworks. Accordingly, interpretive determinability is meant not to eventuate in numerically separate and distinct artworks. Put otherwise, the fact that an artwork might answer to incongruent interpretations (in virtue of its indeterminacy as to nature) does not mandate pluralizing the work into correspondingly separate and distinct works.

But our question remains. How, in light of the thesis of the flux, can the determinability of a cultural object's nature *not* affect its number? And why not say that one cannot say that it answers to one or more interpretations (that it is undecidable) rather than say that—in virtue of the determinability of properties as to nature—it answers to more than one interpretation?

Now, if the distinction between number and nature cannot be sustained, interpretability as to nature would entail pluralizing as to number. The question arises whether the numerical identity of an object can be held fixed in face of its determinability as to nature.

Margolis's thesis of pan-fluxism tends toward the conclusion that determinability as to nature entails determinability as to number. So until Margolis can show that his pan-fluxism does not threaten his central distinction between number and nature, and that determinability as to nature does not entail determinability as to number, his answer amounts to hopeful insistence.

The thesis of the flux does not by itself entail multiplism. The thesis that there are no *de re* necessities, that all necessities are nested within a variant world, is consistent with the view that objects of interpretation change not only in their nature but in their number as well. It is consistent with the possibility that for a given object of interpretation there is a one–one match between it and an interpretation of it.

Finally, while Margolis affirms both the claim of determinability and the claim of multiple determinability (i.e., alternativity), these claims are independent of one another. The thesis of interpretability alone does not entail multiple interpretability. One could allow that interpretive activity alters an entity's nature and that by so doing the entity's number is correspondingly altered. Singularism would obtain if the claim of determinability as to nature were coupled with the claim that there is one and only one admissible way to impute properties as to nature. Multiplism would obtain if determinability as to nature were coupled with the claim that there is more than one admissible way to impute properties as to nature, assuming that such imputation does not necessitate pluralizing the object in question.

As in the parallel cases of Harré, Harrison and Hanna, Wallner, Putnam, and Gupta, Margolis's alternativity of imputing interpretations does not entail multiplism, since a singularist might well argue that, even if imputationism be granted, without a suitable theory of identity the singularity of that which is interpreted cannot be fixed. Let us now turn to the question of identity and related issues of indeterminacy.

NOTES

1. See, for example, Joseph Margolis, *The Truth about Relativism* (Oxford: Basil Blackwell, 1991); "Genres, Laws, Canons, Principles," in ed. Mette Hjort, *Rules and Conventions* (Baltimore, Md.: Johns Hopkins University Press, 1992); and *The Flux of History and the Flux of Science* (Los Angeles: University of California Press, 1993).

2. Margolis, *The Truth about Relativism,* 6.

3. Joseph Margolis, *Interpretation, Radical But Not Unruly: The New Puzzle of the Arts and History* (Berkeley: University of California Press, 1994), 91.

4. Joseph Margolis, "Relativism and Cultural Relativity," *JTLA, Journal of the Faculty of Letters, University of Tokyo, Aesthetics,* 22 (1997), 12–13. Abbreviated as "RCR."

5. With permission from the publisher, portions of the above account are taken from my article, "Interpretation, Relativism, and Culture: Four Questions for Margolis," in ed. Michael Krausz and Richard Shusterman, *Interpretation, Relativism, and the Metaphysics of Culture* (Amherst, N.Y.: Humanity Press, 1999), 105–24.

6. Joseph Margolis, "Reconciling Relativism and the Cultural Realism," *JTLA, Journal of the Faculty of Letters, The University of Tokyo, Aesthetics,* 22 (1997), 79. Abbreviated as "RRCR."

7. Margolis, RRCR, 80.

8. Margolis, RRCR, 82–83.

9. Margolis, RRCR, 83.

10. Margolis, *The Flux of History and the Flux of Science,* 181.

11. Margolis, RRCR, 90.

12. Margolis, RRCR, 87–88.

13. Margolis, RRCR, 89.

14. Margolis, RCR, 10–11.

15. Margolis, RRCR, 92.

16. Margolis, *The Truth about Relativism,* 19–20.

17. Margolis, RRCR, 85.

18. Margolis, RRCR, 83.

19. Margolis, RRCR, 89.

20. Margolis, RRCR, 84.

21. Margolis, RRCR, 84.

22. Margolis, RCR, 17.

Chapter Ten

Questions about Indeterminacy and Identity

In the last chapter I considered Margolis's suggestions that indeterminate cultural objects are on that account multiply interpretable and that imputation may change pertinent properties of one and the same object of interpretation. Two central questions arise. (I) Does the indeterminacy of an interpreted object mandate its multiple interpretability? And (II) does a change in an object's properties—whether or not by imputation—mandate a change in its identity? Answers to both of these questions bear on the very applicability of singularism and multiplism. I shall take up these questions in turn. As regards (I), I offer two examples: the works of Christo and historical processes in general.

I

Consider Christo's Wrapped Reichstag in Berlin in 1995. It is an indeterminate object of interpretation. This is what Stephen Kinzer said about it in 1994 before its realization.

The artist is Christo, famous for wrapping Florida islands in pink plastic; late last month, after a 22-year quest, he won permission to wrap the Reichstag in a million square feet of silver fiber for two weeks next year, as a symbol of the passing of one era and the beginning of another. . . . The legislators who approved it have more in mind than attracting attention (and tourists) to Berlin: They hope for a kind of exorcism of ghosts, knowing that this building, which carries the name of Germany's first national parliament, symbolizes like no other the heights and depths of German history. . . . Last month, the Reichstag was again the subject of heated debate as Parliament considered Christo's proposal to wrap it. Ultimately, it was approved over Chancellor Kohl's objections—in the hope that when the fabric is removed, the building will re-emerge not only as the center of a modern

new Government complex, but as a symbol of Germany's long-thwarted desire to
build a united, peaceful and stable democracy.[1]

We may ask, What is Christo's work? What is "it"? Is "it" the dour German
Parliament building that came to be wrapped with 60.5 tons of billowing sil-
very fabric held in place by 10 miles of bright blue rope? Is "it" more than
"the hulking, bombastic building . . . transformed into an airy and evanescent
form" that Michael Kimmelman describes? After the completion of Wrapped
Reichstag, Kimmelman said:

> "It" means the whole giddy affair—the revelers who turned the bleak fields
> around the Reichstag into Woodstock East, the art students who gathered to
> sketch the building, the street vendors, the posturing politicos, the store windows
> around Berlin suddenly filled with wrapped objects, and the billboards that used
> the project to hawk beer and cigarettes.[2]

Kimmelman says of the completed project, "It left an afterimage of a
kinder, gentler Reichstag. I, for one, can't imagine seeing it, or Berlin, the
same way again." Is part of the work the afterimages of those who saw the
wrapped Reichstag? Christo, who himself thinks of his projects as consisting
of what happens from concept to realization and to its effects beyond, might
well have included Kimmelman's afterimages in his work. So understood, we
may say that Christo's work is indeterminate in the sense that there are no
clear boundary conditions that distinguish between what is *internal* to it and
what is *external* to it.

Such indeterminacy is also found in numerous other characteristic works of
Christo, including his "Valley Curtain," a huge orange curtain drawn across a
Colorado valley. It prompts the following questions. What are the boundary
conditions of Christo's work, "Valley Curtain"? Is Christo's work the orange
curtain that is drawn across the Colorado valley? Or is it the natural *landscape* that the curtain frames? Or is it the *idea* that a gigantic curtain drawn
in a natural environment may count as a work of art? Or is it the *thought* that
what makes an artwork an artwork the fact of designating or circumscribing
a physical space? Or is the artwork is the very *staging* and *managing* of the
event? Or, is it the *spoof* on the very idea of an artwork, that, just as it does
not apply in the valley, by extension it does not apply in the museum? Or is
it the *point* that each of these possibilities may be plausibly defended—which
leads to the further possibility that the *debate* about the possibilities of possibilities turns out, in turn, to be part of Christo's work? The possibility that the
work may be any or all of these suggests that Christo's works simply have no
determinate boundary conditions.

But one might press for clarification by asking where the indeterminacy
lies. Of a work of Christo one might ask whether (a) it is the *work* (whatever
that is) that is indeterminate, or whether (b) it is the *work as represented* that

is indeterminate, or whether (c) it is indeterminate *which work* is being considered. The suggestion that it is the work as represented that is indeterminate (b) amounts to the claim that the indeterminacy is located in the looseness of expressive devices and not in anything in the work itself. Yet one could agree that indeterminacy applies at the epistemic level and at the same time leave it open whether the object at the ontic level is either determinate or indeterminate. That is, there is no need to foreclose the possibility that, on independent grounds, the object might be either determinate or indeterminate. And the suggestion that indeterminacy concerns which work is being referred to (c) need not amount to a claim about indeterminacy in a work or in referring expressions. Accordingly, from the fact that people might disagree about the boundary conditions of cultural achievements (b) it does not follow that such entities themselves are indeterminate (a). They could just be talking about different things (c). We should not confuse the fact that people disagree about what they are referring to, with the referents *being* indeterminate.

But the Christo examples resist the disambiguations suggested by distinguishing between (a), (b), and (c). What is so interesting about Christo's works is that the works as mentioned in (a), and the works as represented in (b), and the distinctions between works as mentioned in (c) are run together. Perhaps this fact signals that the pertinent distinctions apply to some genres and not to others. But the kinds of works that are characteristically said to be indeterminate are, as Margolis mentions, such things as paintings of Klee or Kiefer, or the musical works of Brahms, and so on, where the distinctions in (a), (b), and (c) do seem to apply. And it is with such cultural entities in mind that Margolis ties the claim that cultural entities are determinable with the claim that they are multiply interpretable. His suggestion is that their indeterminacy as in (a) and/or (b) grounds their answering to multiplism.

So understood, I suggest that an object of interpretation might be indeterminate but it might nevertheless still answer to one and only one ideally admissible interpretation, perhaps where the pertinent interpretation itself allows for a corresponding indeterminacy. Under such a condition, indeterminacy of an object of interpretation would not mandate multiplism. Alternatively, when the indeterminacy is such that the identity of the object of interpretation cannot be sufficiently fixed, one just cannot say if it answers *at all* to either one or more contending interpretations. In such a case it would be best to withhold judgment as to the applicability of singularism or multiplism. Either way, the indeterminacy of an object of interpretation does not mandate multiplism.

Consider the indeterminacy of historical processes. The possibility that indeterminacy exists at the epistemic level only (as in (b)) is foreclosed in the case of historical processes. R. G. Collingwood observes that

> history is concerned not with 'events' but with 'processes'; that 'processes' are things which do not begin and end but turn into one another; and that if a process

P1 turns into a process P2, there is no dividing line at which P1 stops and P2 begins; P1 never stops, it goes on in the changed form P2, and P2 never begins, it has previously been going on in the earlier form P1. There are in history no beginnings and no endings. History books begin and end, but the events they describe do not. . . . Therefore, if the symbol P1 stands for a characteristic of a certain historical period and the symbol P2 for the corresponding but different (and therefore contradictory or incompatible) characteristic of its successor, that successor is never characterized by P2 pure and simple, but always by a P2 tinged with a survival of P1. This is why people who try to depict the characteristic features of this or that historical period go wrong if they do their work too thoroughly, forgetting that the silk of their period is in reality always a shot silk, combining in itself contradictory colours.³

Collingwood's thought is that historical processes are indeterminate in the sense that they exhibit "no dividing line at which P1 stops and P2 begins." (He might have extended the point to cover all processes.) Yet realist Gail Soffer mistakenly demands determinacy of historical events when she argues that

the counterfactual activity of the imagination directs us towards a reality which can be determinate and univocal *beyond* the bounds and multiplicities of our interpretations.⁴

Soffer ramifies her point with the aid of a distinction between *evidential indeterminacy* and *intentional determinacy*. More fully, she says:

Granted that certain features of history may be phenomenologically nebulous . . . there remain other features which are constituted as relatively determinate, and here again essential counterfactual elements are included in the very meaning of truth, guaranteeing its univocity and constancy through various interpretations. For example, when we affirm that something "really" happened in the past, an essential part of what we mean is that, for example, if someone capable of perceiving the event had been there, he or she would have witnessed it. This claim is in principle unverifiable, and yet it is precisely the counterfactual activity of the imagination that gives the experience of directness towards something determinable and decidable, what "really" (bivalently) happened (e.g., something I would have seen if I had been there). Thus, we have at once *evidential* indeterminacy (the evidence is insufficient to be conclusive across different interpretive backgrounds), but *intentional* determinacy (we remain directed towards a truth which is in principle but not in practice uniquely and intersubjectively determinable).⁵

Soffer thinks that whatever indeterminacies might be found in history must be attributable to an epistemic lack. Consequently, evidential indeterminacy must give way to "the counterfactual activity of the imagination that gives the experience of directness towards something determinable and decidable, what 'really' (bivalently) happened (e.g., something I would have seen if I had been there)." Evidential indeterminacy must give way to intentional determinacy. But even for a realist it does not follow that "what really happened" need be determinate. Put otherwise, evidential indeterminacy may give way to *either* intentional determinacy *or* indeterminacy. Nothing in realism as such mandates that that which is taken as real must be determinate. Even being there does not ensure "intentional determinacy."

Correspondingly, there is no reason why a constructivist or a constructive realist should require that objects of history should be determinate. Neither realism nor constructivism nor constructive realism entails the determinacy of their interpreted objects. And from the claim that an object of interpretation is indeterminate, again, it follows neither that it answers to singularism, to multiplism, nor to either.

And determinacy is not required for self-identity. An indeterminate thing can be identified and re-identified as the thing that it is. Even physical objects may be indeterminate and identified and reidentified as the objects they are. For example, with each microscopic blow-up or "zoom" of such an object as a stick, say, one finds levels of indeterminacy. The boundaries of the object are indeterminate. The fact that the range of indeterminacy might be progressively narrowed might suggest that there is a convergence to a determinate limit. Yet the fact of progressive convergence is compatible with *there being no* completely determinate limit. Indeed, however infinitesimally small the range of indeterminacy becomes, there may always remain a range of indeterminacy. At the same time, even when the stick is zoomed indefinitely and reveals its indeterminacies at each zoom, one typically continues to call the zooms zooms of the *same* stick. But this fact of indeterminacy does not mandate that the object answers to either one or more interpretations. Whether the object answers to singularism or multiplism depends upon the fit between it and the considered interpretation(s). The indeterminacy of an object does not entail multiplism, for there may well be a one–one match between the object of interpretation (with its indeterminacy) and a single admissible interpretation (with complementing indeterminacy of its own). And this point is unique to neither realism, constructivism, nor constructive realism. So the tie between indeterminacy and multiplism is not a necessary one.

II

I turn to the question of whether pertinent properties of an object of interpretation can be changed *while remaining one and the same* object of interpretation. If with such change of property there is change in the identity of the object, a multiplist condition would not obtain. That is, multiplism requires that it is one and the same object of interpretation that competing interpretations address. And with no such commonality an innocuous pluralism rather than a multiplism would obtain.

One might hold that no particular commitments are made about the identity of an object by saying that the object endures over time. That is, by saying, for example, that "that boat in Angler's boatyard this season is the same boat as was there last season" is not to say that any or all of its properties are taken as fixing its identity. So understood, "that boat" would function as a placeholder expression. But if one does take some, or all, or an arrangement of its properties as fixing identity, several possibilities arise. Accordingly, I offer four such views of identity.

First, one might hold (1) that *all* properties of an object fix its identity, that a change in any of its properties entails a change in the identity of the object. This view of identity is clearly too strong, for it rules out that any self-same thing could change over time. It rules out that a boat that is being painted, for example, could be the self-same boat. If we do allow that under these conditions the boat could be the self-same boat we should disallow (1). Otherwise as one paints the boat, different boats would obtain. Not *all* of an object's properties should be taken to fix its identity.

Alternatively, consider the thought (2) that a subclass of properties of an object fixes its identity, that is, its "essential" properties serve as a criterion for its identity. Accordingly, not all of a thing's properties need be invariant for it to remain the self-same thing. Object a at time t-1 can be the same a at t-2 if the essential properties of a at t-1 are the same essential properties of a at t-2. Consequently, a might take on (or off) certain properties (whether or not by imputation) and still remain self-identical. Accordingly, (2) amounts to the claim that any change in the essential properties of an object would entail a change in the identity of the object, but a change in nonessential properties would not. For example, according to (2) when one walks on the beach and picks up a pebble and puts it into one's pocket, the added nonessential property of *ownership* does not alter its identity. While the pebble takes on a new property, it is not an essential property, one that enters into the conditions that fix the pebble's identity.

But doubts emerge about (2) when we consider that there may be circumstances under which ownership is not to be regarded as nonessential, that the distinction between essential and non-essential depends upon context of use. If the pebble were especially valued, say, for its special chemical composition in the context of a demanding market, its new ownership might indeed come to be seen as essential.

This leads us to the thought that perhaps no properties of a thing could *inherently* fix its identity. As Wittgenstein asks, "But where are the bounds of the incidental?"[6]

Third, consider the thought (3) that a thing may be a self-same thing at different instances without even holding fixed essential properties. Wittgenstein champions this possibility when considering what might be "common" in two instances when he says:

Consider for example the proceedings that we call "games." I mean board-games, card-games, ball-games, Olympic games, and so on. What is common between them?—Don't say: "There *must* be something common, or they would not be called 'games'"—but *look and see* whether there is anything in common to *all.*—For if you look at them you will not see something that is common to all, but similarities, relationships, and a whole series of them at that. To repeat: don't think, but look!—Look for example at board-games, with their multifarious relationships. Now pass to card-games; here you may find many correspondences with the first group, but many features drop out, and others appear. When we pass next to ball-games, much that is in common is retained, but much is lost.

And the result of this examination is: we see a complicated network of similarities overlapping and criss-crossing sometimes overall similarities, sometimes similarities of detail.[7]

And Wittgenstein asks:

Has the name "Moses" got a fixed and unequivocal use for me in all possible cases?—Is it not the case that I have, so to speak, a whole series of props in readiness, and am ready to lean on one if another should be taken from under me and vice versa?[8]

Wittgenstein's point is quite general, as evidenced in his further remark:

But similar doubts to those about "Moses" are possible about the words of this explanation (what are you calling "Egypt," whom the "Israelites" etc.?). Nor would these questions come to an end when we got down to words like "red," "dark," "sweet."—"But then how does an explanation help me to understand, if after all it is not the final one? In that case the explanation is never completed; so I still don't understand what he means, and never shall!"—As though an explanation as it were hung in the air unless supported by another one. Whereas an explanation may indeed rest on another one that has been given, but none stands in need of another—unless *we* require it to prevent a misunderstanding.[9]

J. J. Gibson perspicuously summarizes Wittgenstein's approach to identity when he says:

you *cannot* specify the necessary and sufficient features of the class of things to which a name is given. They have only a "family resemblance." But this does not mean you cannot learn how to use things and perceive their uses. You do not have to classify and label things in order to perceive what they afford.[10]

And Harré concurs and ramifies the thought when he says in this passage:

In English 'same' comprehends both numerical identity (one and the same) and qualitative identity (exactly similar). A study of identity must include discussions of the criteria by which judgments of each kind of identity are routinely made about individuals in . . . some field of human endeavor. There are many complications and variations in the criteria in use and in their modes of applications. . . . 'Same litre of milk' and 'same sum of money' differ in that the former requires the preservation of one and the same substance while the latter requires only the preservation of abstract numerical value. Electron identity may be more like monetary identity than like lactic identity. And, as Wittgenstein demonstrated . . . the concept of 'same pain' is not explicated in terms of either qualitative or numerical identity, but rather in the similarities and differences in the ways in which being in pains fits into the pattern of a person's public and private life.

In his treatment of bodily feelings Wittgenstein shows that 'same pain again' is neither individuated nor re-identified by the use of criteria of numerical identity and qualitative identity like those we would use for 'same table again' in being seated in a restaurant. Repeated occurrences of a pain can neither be juxtaposed to one another for point by point comparison, nor be compared with a common exemplar. Nor can my pain be compared with yours except in so far as our expression of a pain are [sic] similar or dissimilar. A pain is not a thing but, says Wittgenstein, 'it is not a nothing either.' The notion of 'same pain' has an important part to play in our lives. Its use is governed by rules that relate the common means of the expression of the pain to the public and private contexts in which they are routinely employed.[11]

The family resemblance view (3) allows that a thing's properties might be thought of as "threads in the fabric" of the thing, so to say, no one thread being essential for it to be the self-same fabric. In (3) no given condition is taken to be invariantly essential.

Yet in opposition to (3), one might hold that the family resemblance view of identity is no view of identity at all. Rather, it is a view about resemblance. That is, one should not confuse a theory of resemblance with a theory of identity. But here one must be careful not to beg the question. That is, a Wittgensteinian remark that a theory of identity that takes all or any of an object's specific properties as fixing its identity is too strong, is a remark about a theory of identity. Whether or not one agrees with it, it will not do to say that it is not about identity. The family resemblance view is an answer to the question, What softer conditions than all-or-some properties should be invoked for identity? The dismissal of the family resemblance view of identity as not really about identity presupposes precisely the conditions of adequacy that the family resemblance view is meant to critique.

Notice that the essential properties view (2) and the family resemblance view (3) allow for (but do not entail) imputationism, since properties might be added (or subtracted) by means of imputation or by some other means. Yet it remains that even according to (3), things *can* change their identities, if not by changes in what would otherwise be defined by (2) as essential.

Yet a fourth possibility arises, one we may dub "reconstructivist." That is, in the course of a concept's career, essential properties may be substituted by other essential properties. That is, *for a given stage* of a career an object is definable in terms of certain essential properties. Yet one might ask how it can be that it is one and the same entity that endures throughout the stages of "its" career? In other words, if "essential" is not invariant, then how can one know that it is the same entity that is instantiated in its various stages? A reconstructivist might answer that what is identified as essential to an entity at one stage may be revised in light of a post hoc narrative of its career. What is taken to be essential to it may be a product of a post hoc narratizing of the career, which either does or does not recognize the previously taken essential properties as essential. And what is taken as essential is a matter of negotiation. Put otherwise, identity may be preserved while essential properties are replaced in virtue of a post hoc narratizing of what belongs to the career of the sorting concept of the pertinent entity. And that is a matter of negotiation by pertinent practitioners. The entity is counted as the same in virtue of a revision in the conception of the sort of thing it is, despite its essential properties having been shifted. What is taken as essential is an invention of a post hoc narrative, and with a change in the narrative may come a change in essential properties.

But the reconstructivist faces the objection that his or her position does not show that essential conditions of an entity actually have been substituted. On the contrary, the initially identified essential conditions at the initial stage might have been mistakenly so identified. That is, a reconstruction would bring a correction of an initially mistaken identification of essential conditions. It would not be the case that subsequent identified essential conditions are of the "same thing."

We may recast the same point in other terms. One might well concede that, *for a given stage* of a career, an object is definable in terms of certain essential properties. Essentiality may be nested in a broadly fluxist ontology, where essentiality is understood only locally. Accordingly, the local specification of essentiality would be compatible with the Wittgensteinian option (3). Yet, even with this modified use of essentiality as nested in a variant and noninherent landscape, the question arises how it can be that it is the same object that endures throughout the stages of an object's career. If essentiality is not invariant, then how can one know that it is the same object that is instantiated in its various stages? Note that there is question begging on both sides of this issue. On the one hand, one may assume that invariance is required to establish sameness. And on the other hand, one who responds by saying that a given object may be instantiated in different stages of its career despite a shift in essential properties presumes that the career is a career of the self-same object. I offer no solution to this standoff. But for present purposes I need none, for my concern is to show that singularism and multiplism require commonality of object as addressed by possibly contending interpretations—*whichever* account of commonality ultimately triumphs.

CHANGING THE SUBJECT

When different objects do obtain, an interesting sort of discourse arises as to which resulting object should be interpreted. Where otherwise contesting interpretations do not address a common object of interpretation, one may critically discuss which of the different objects of interpretation one *should* address as the proper object, one that might better serve one's interests. That is, one might change the focus of the inquiry from the question, "Which of competing interpretations of the same thing should we embrace?" to "To what object of interpretation should we address ourselves?" In the conduct of inquiry this amounts to a significantly different stance than has been pursued. So far we have spoken of pluralism as if it is philosophically innocuous in that no conflict could arise when different interpretations address different things. But once one concedes that different interpretations may address different objects it is a matter of great importance as to which object one *should* take as the object of inquiry. That is, which subject is chosen, or whether the subject *should* be changed can be a matter of great significance. The dissolution of a case that initially appears to be multiplist into a pluralist case might first appear to be innocuous, but the subsequent question as to how to deal with the pluralized object of interpretation may be not all that innocuous.

I have noted that cultural achievements, historical processes, and physical objects may be indeterminate but self-identical. And their indeterminacy is compatible with singularism, multiplism, or neither. Further, whether a pluralist or multiplist condition obtains depends upon an assumed account of the identity of the object of interpretation. I have set aside as implausible the view that all properties of an object are defining of it. And I have further distinguished the view that holds that some properties are essential to an object, from the Wittgensteinian family resemblance view, and in turn from a reconstructivist view. As regards the contest between these latter views I leave the matter open. In any event, the overriding point is that identity—however understood—is a necessary condition for the applicability of singularism or multiplism.

NOTES

1. Stephen Kinzer, "Berlin's Symbol of Hope and Agony Awaits a New Ordeal: Tinsel," *New York Times,* Sunday, March 6, 1994, E5.

2. Michael Kimmelman, "It Was Big, It Was Fun and That's Enough," *New York Times*, July 1995, 26.

3. R. G. Collingwood, *An Autobiography* (Oxford: Clarendon, 1939), 97–98.

4. Gail Soffer, "Relativity, Intentionality, and the 'Puzzle' of Interpretation," in ed._Michael Krausz and Richard Shusterman, *Interpretation, Relativism and the Metaphysics of Culture* (Amherst, N.Y.: Humanity Press, 1999), 72.

5. Soffer, "Relativity, Intentionality, and the 'Puzzle' of Interpretation," 71.

6. Ludwig Wittgenstein, *Philosophical Investigations* (Oxford: Basil Blackwell, 1958), §79, 37.

7. Wittgenstein, *Philosophical Investigations,* §66, 31–32.

8. Wittgenstein, *Philosophical Investigations,* *§*79, 37.

9. Wittgenstein, *Philosophical Investigations*, §87, 40–41.

10. J. J. Gibson, *The Ecological Approach to Visual Perception* (Hillsdale, N.J.: Lawrence Erlbaum, 1986), 134.

11. Rom Harré, "Is There a Basic Ontology for the Physical Sciences?" *Dialectica,* 51, Fasc. 1 (1997), 32–33.

Chapter Eleven

Aims of Interpretation

One argument that has been offered for multiplism is the argument from the multiplicity of interpretive aims. It holds that different interpretations are admissible if each addresses distinct aims. When advancing the multiple-aims argument for multiplism Robert Stecker, for example, says that "acceptability varies with the aim of the interpreter and . . . there are many legitimate aims with which we interpret."[1] And he denies that "there is one dominant aim of interpretation."[2] This view raises a number of interesting issues. One concerns whether the putative multiple aims are conjoinable into one aim. Another concerns whether they are aims of *interpretation*. A still further issue is whether speaking of aims of interpretation requires an essentialist construal of interpretation. To anticipate, I shall suggest that, while aims are interest-relative, even if there is a diversity of aims, multiplism is not thereby entailed.

I offer two general sorts of aims that one might take to be aims of interpretation. I distinguish between *elucidation* and *edification*. By an elucidatory aim I mean an aim that in general terms (as the *Oxford English Dictionary* indicates) seeks to render lucid, to explain, to make intelligible, or to make sense of or to understand a work. In contrast, by an edificatory aim I mean an aim that seeks (again, as the *Oxford English Dictionary* indicates) to build character, to impart moral or spiritual stability, or the like. Edificatory aims may be of an individual or a collective kind. They typically include (individual) emancipatory concerns such as those found in programs of self-development, soteriologies toward personal emancipation, or (collective) cultural or historical reconciliations, or the like.

The aims of elucidation and edification are not so broad as to lack content, for elucidation and edification are distinguishable from one another. In the analogous case of science, for example, the broad aim may be taken to be explanation. And the fact that it has such sub-aims as predictability,

113

management of information, and the like does not render the broad aim of explanation void of content.

With these broad aims in mind we can distinguish three views: (a) Interpretation has a single intrinsic aim and it is elucidation. (b) Interpretation has a multiplicity of intrinsic aims, and that includes elucidation and edification. And (c) interpretation has no intrinsic aims, but may be assigned one aim or more aims depending upon one's interests. I call these three views, respectively, (a) the intrinsic single-aim view, (b) the intrinsic multiple-aims view, and (c) the nonintrinsic interest-relative view. According to the intrinsic single-aim view interpretation has one *intrinsic* aim, although other aims may be extrinsic and may be pursued simultaneously. And that one intrinsic aim is the elucidation of objects of interpretation.

Consider two examples where the aims of elucidation and edification appear. In chapter 2 I considered the German paintings of Anselm Kiefer and (in an elucidatory mode) I asked if they answer to *exorcist* or *celebratory* interpretations or perhaps both. Now, according to the intrinsic single-aim view, the single aim of these interpretations is elucidatory. It is to make sense of Kiefer's paintings. At the same time, this intrinsic single-aim view allows that interpretation might be *used* to further a distinct extrinsic aim, namely the edification of receivers. Such extrinsic edification may involve for receivers, as the case may be, their reconciliation with German history or their perpetuation of Nazi values. In either case such a further aim would not count as an aim of interpretation as such. That is, if one were to champion the exorcist or the celebratory interpretations *in order to* contribute toward one's agenda of reconciling oneself with German history, or *in order to* promote the values of its Nazi past, then one would be *using* interpretation in pursuit of an aim extrinsic to interpretation.

Let us consider how the intrinsic single-aim view would be applied to a particular commentary on Kiefer's paintings. Jungian psychotherapist Rafael Lopez-Pedraza, for example, offers the following account. He says:

> Anselm Kiefer seems to be representative of a new generation of German artists who are painfully aware of the terrible history they have inherited. Kiefer reflects the suffering brought about by the pressure of the German complexes and brings a historical perspective not only to his own tragedy, but also that of his country and Western culture. . . . Through a retrograde movement of the psyche, he reaches a symmetry with the contents he pursues. Kiefer mobilizes his imaginative creativity by way of a regression into the historical past. I contend that we must view such a regression in the Jungian sense, namely, as a search for oneself. In the case of Kiefer, part of the search for himself is through Germany's historical past and its collective unconscious, within himself. . . . From the beginning, Kiefer was deeply aware of the importance of what he was doing, both for Germany's historical memory and for the processes of artistic creativity.[3]

Lopez-Pedraza also takes Kiefer's paintings as evidence of Kiefer's individual therapy when he says:

> I consider Kiefer's art a great achievement in individuation, meaning that he has dealt successfully with unconscious contents of the sort that have most proved to induce identification. The psychological reflections conveyed by Kiefer's work as a whole reveal an unparalleled individuation, one that enables his psyche to withstand the powerful forces of the strong German unconscious.[4]

Now, the intrinsic single-aim view would allow that Lopez-Pedraza seeks to *elucidate* the works by indicating the intentional context of Kiefer's production. Lopez-Pedraza fills in the intentional context that helps to elucidate the works. Yet Lopez-Pedraza further speculates that Kiefer's approach might satisfy an extrinsic aim—and he applauds Kiefer for it—when he says that Kiefer's approach does have "a healing effect on the Germans."[5]

The intrinsic single-aim view would have it that, if Kiefer's paintings are taken to embody a reconciliationist effort on *his* part, in order for *us receivers* to make sense of his efforts, Kiefer's individual and cultural concerns should indeed factor into one's account of Kiefer's paintings. That would satisfy the intrinsic elucidatory aim of interpretation. But if Lopez-Pedraza himself were to favor the exorcist interpretation *in order to* facilitate the "healing effect on the Germans" he would be *using* interpretive activity in an extrinsic way. According to the intrinsic single-aim view of interpretation, the edification of a receiver is not an aim of interpretation as such. Put otherwise, one's concern for the reconciliation of German history, say, might prompt one's actually embracing the exorcist over the celebratory interpretation, where these interpretations are first offered in an elucidatory mode. But according to the intrinsic single-aim view that would satisfy an aim that is extrinsic to the aim of interpretation. Accordingly, *to use interpretation to satisfy certain aims is not to make those aims the aims of interpretation.*

Let us consider how the intrinsic single-aim view would be applied in consideration of another sort of case. Consider two soteriologies that seek to elucidate the "nature of things" generally understood, *and* they seek to provide edificatory or emancipatory paths toward realization or liberation. Hinduism and Buddhism are offered in order to elucidate the nature of things in general and to edify or emancipate one from what each diagnoses as mental infliction. The Hindu soteriology, for example, seeks At-Oneness with the Cosmic Self, the Atma. It seeks that aim when prescribing such mantras as "Thou Art That," or "I am Infinite, I am Bliss." In turn, the Buddhist mantra, "Om mani padme hum," means, as the Dalai Lama says, "that in dependence on the practice of a path which is an indivisible union of method and wisdom, you can transform your impure body, speech, and mind into the pure exalted body, speech, and body of a Buddha."[6] Such mantras are meant simultaneously to satisfy elucidatory and emancipatory aims. Both Hinduism and Buddhism take their meditative practices to satisfy both aims. Now the pursuit of the aims of elucidation and edification may come in stages. At one stage a Hindu, for example, may aim toward the elucidation of the nature of things as a prelude to pursuing the aim of emancipation. Or conversely, one's ability to elucidate may be enhanced by advancement in one's emancipatory journey. In other words, these aims may be in symbiosis. Again, a proponent of the intrinsic single-aim view would affirm that interpretation as such is elucidatory. Accordingly, the fact that the aims of elucidation and edification might be in symbiosis would not be taken to mean that both aims are aims of *interpretation*. According to the intrinsic single-aim view, the pursuit of emancipation of the receiver would reflect an aim extrinsic to interpretation. Insofar as one aim of Hinduism and Buddhism is elucidatory—in seeking to make sense of the nature of things generally—they indeed seek to fulfill the aim of interpretation. And the intrinsic single-aim view still allows that the pursuit of the edificatory aim may, at different stages, be regarded as more or less important than the elucidatory aim, perhaps depending upon one's stage on one's soteriological path. In sum, according to the intrinsic single-aim view, edification could extrinsically *use* elucidatory interpretation, but edification would not count as an aim of interpretation as such.

Now consider the intrinsic single-aim view in relation to an intrinsic multiple-aims view that would allow that more aims than one are intrinsic to interpretation. The intrinsic multiple-aims view would include elucidation *and* edification. It would hold that the claim advanced by the intrinsic single-aim view that the edificatory aim is extrinsic to interpretation is too restrictive.

Stecker, for example, enumerates several other possible aims of interpretation when he articulates his multiple-aims argument. Note that Stecker does not characterize his own list of possible aims of interpretation as "intrinsic" to interpretation. But the list can help to articulate the intrinsic multiple-aims view. He says:

> the acceptability of an interpretation is relative to the aim with which it is advanced or received, and there are numerous candidates for reasonable interpretive aims. Sometimes we aim at understanding a work as the product of the intentional activity of the historically situated artist. Sometimes we aim merely at finding *an* understanding of a work, one that makes sense of its parts, as parts of a whole, in a way that promotes appreciation. Sometimes we aim at maximizing the aesthetic value of the work or a particular encounter with it. Sometimes we aim at making the work relevant to a particular audience. Some interpretations even aim at creating a work in collaboration with the original artist.[7]

The proponent of the intrinsic multiple-aims view would affirm that there is a multiplicity of aims of *interpretation*. Stecker comments, "Sometimes we aim at understanding a work as the product of the intentional activity of the historically situated artist." The intrinsic single-aim proponent would understand such an activity as falling under the more general aim of elucidation. Stecker goes on to list several more candidates. He says, "Sometimes we aim merely at finding *an* understanding of a work, one that makes sense of its parts, as parts of a whole, in a way that promotes appreciation." The intrinsic single-aim proponent would count this candidate also as falling under the general elucidatory aim of interpretation—if, that is, "the promotion of appreciation" is taken as an invitation to *elucidate* a work, perhaps by making sense of its parts as parts of a whole, as Stecker says. But if by "appreciation" one means something like maximizing pleasure, then, an intrinsic single-aim proponent would take the aim of maximizing pleasure as an aim *distinct* from the elucidatory aim. And although maximizing pleasure is often associated with interpretation, the intrinsic single-aim view would hold that that it is not *intrinsic* to the aim of interpretation. Indeed, sometimes it is an open question whether interpretation does enhance pleasure or enjoyment. The intrinsic single-aim view allows that one may be *motivated* to engage in interpretive activity with the hope or the expectation that it might yield pleasure. But whether it does so or not, such a motive is *extrinsic* to the aim of interpretation, which is elucidatory. So, according to the intrinsic single-aim view it would be an extrinsic *use* of interpretation to maximize "the aesthetic value of the work or a particular encounter with it," or to make "the work relevant to a particular audience." In short, the intrinsic single-aim view of interpretation holds that there is a single aim of interpretation, and it is elucidation. And this does not preclude the simultaneous pursuit of extrinsic aims.

Notice that the intrinsic multiple-aims view allows that with respect to each intrinsic aim there may be either one or more than one ideally admissible interpretation. That is, the intrinsic multiple-aims view allows that, with respect to elucidation, there are *one or more* admissible interpretations of a pertinent object. And the intrinsic multiple-aims view allows that with respect to edification, there are *one or more* admissible interpretations of a pertinent object.

Much, of course, depends upon how one counts aims. For the intrinsic multiple-aims argument to work *the pertinent aims should not be conjoinable into a single aim. Otherwise, the aims would not be multiple. There must be some pertinent "opposition" that precludes their conjunction.* At the same time the opposition should not be so strong as to disallow all but one aim. They should be opposed but not exclusive. To recall our discussion in chapter 1, if they were exclusive and one of the aims were admissible, the other(s) would be rejected as inadmissible.

Further, in order for either the intrinsic single-aim or the intrinsic multiple-aims argument to go through, the aims would have to be aims of *interpretation.* That is why it is important to introduce the thought that if there is a single aim or if there are multiple aims they should be *intrinsic* to interpretation. But one might object that the distinction between intrinsic and extrinsic must be grounded in an essentialism, and on independent grounds such essentialism is objectionable. In brief, the doctrine of essentialism holds that a thing is (in this case an interpretive aim is) what it is in virtue of its embodying an "essence" whose properties are inherent and invariant. (A fuller treatment of essentialism will be found in chapter 13.)

Yet despite our embracing a broadly antiessentialist stance one could still speak of what is intrinsic and extrinsic to interpretation. To see this more clearly consider the classic antiessentialist statement of Morris Weitz, who endorses Wittgenstein's antiessentialism when he says:

> If I may paraphrase Wittgenstein, we must not ask, What is the nature of any philosophical x? or even, according to the semanticist, What does "x" mean? . . . but rather, What is the use or employment of "x"? What does "x" do in the language? This, I take it, is the initial question, the begin-all if not the end-all of any philosophical problem and solution. Thus, in aesthetics, our first problem is the elucidation of the actual employment of the concept of art, to give a logical description of the actual functioning of the concept, including a description of the conditions under which we correctly use it or its correlates.[8]

And Weitz stresses his resistance to essentialism when he says:

> To understand the role of aesthetic theory is . . . to read it as summaries of seriously made recommendations to attend in certain ways to certain features of art.[9]

This antiessentialist stance allows that certain summaries of pertinent practices may specify what is intrinsic and extrinsic to those practices. The deployment of "intrinsic" and "extrinsic" is acceptable if qualified by the denial that the practices in which they operate are construed along essentialist lines. Put otherwise, antiessentialism is consistent with the thought that, within the context of "summaries of seriously made recommendations," certain concepts are indeed defined *locally* in terms of intrinsic conditions. Weitz says further:

> The problem of the nature of art is like that of the nature of games, at least in these respects: If we actually look and see what it is that we call "art," we will also find no common properties—only strands of similarities. Knowing what art is is not apprehending some manifest or latent essence but being able to recognize, describe, and explain those things we call "art" in virtue of these similarities.
>
> But the basic resemblance between these concepts ["art" and "game"] is their open texture. In elucidating them, certain (paradigm) cases can be given, about which there can be no question as to their being correctly described as "art" or "game," but no exhaustive set of cases can be given. I can list some cases and some conditions under which I can apply correctly the concept of art but I cannot list all of them, for the all-important reason that unforeseeable or novel conditions are always forthcoming or envisageable.[10]

Weitz is right to emphasize that knowing what art is (or, for our purposes, what interpretation or its aims are) "is not apprehending some manifest or latent essence but being able to recognize, describe, and explain those things we call 'art' in virtue of pertinent similarities." He is right to emphasize the open texture of such concepts. And that does not disallow that at certain stages in the careers of such concepts certain conditions or aims are taken to be intrinsic and others extrinsic. Otherwise, one could not enumerate what, as Weitz suggests, are "paradigm cases."

In saying that the intrinsic single aim of interpretation is elucidation, one could hold that it is so at a given stage in the career of interpretive practice, leaving it open that in different historical or cultural circumstances it might be different. That is, the nature of interpretive aims may be taken as noninherent and historically variable. If aims of interpretation are understood in this antiessentialist way, it remains an empirical question as to what aims interpreters characteristically seek to satisfy when interpreting. Notice that this antiessentialist stance is not unique to the intrinsic single-aim view. The intrinsic multiple-aims view also allows that some aims are intrinsic to interpretation and some are extrinsic to interpretation. Talk of what aims are intrinsic to interpretation does not in itself mandate single or multiple aims of interpretation.

Having dislodged the connection between essentialism and the intrinsic single-aim view and the intrinsic multiple-aims view, now consider a third view of aims of interpretation, one that holds that whatever aims interpretations might have, they are not intrinsic. In contrast with the view that interpretation either *has* or does *not have* one or more aims, this view holds that an aim depends upon one's interests. That is, given certain interests, an aim of interpretation may be elucidation. Given other interests, it may be edification. And given still other interests, it may include, as Stecker says, the maximizing of "the aesthetic values of the work or a particular encounter with it" or to making "the work relevant to a particular audience."[11] Accordingly, the question of whether interpretation comes to have one or more aims depends upon one's interests. The point is that interpretation *as such* has no aims, but may come to have aims in virtue of one's interests. Another way of stating the interest-relative view is to say that interpretation is itself not a substantive kind or sort. That is, one can use the activity of interpretation one way or another depending upon one's interests. Interpretations independent of the context of interests have no aims as such.

Clearly the interest-relative view side-steps the issue of essentialism altogether. But even the interest-relative view of aims needs to discriminate what, with respect to designated interests, is pertinent to interpretive activity and what is not. According to the interest-relative view of aims, elucidation may remain the single aim of interpretation if, as an anthropological fact, elucidation is what interpreters are characteristically interested in seeking in interpretive activity. Under these conditions elucidation would stand alone as the aim of interpretation.

Finally does the multiple-aims argument—whether or not intrinsic—actually support multiplism? Recall that the multiplist condition obtains when a given object of interpretation answers to more than one incongruent admissible interpretation. And the pluralizing strategy with respect to objects of interpretation is a strategy whereby what initially appears to be a single object is found to be a plurality of objects. That is, the would-be self-same object of interpretation turns out to be distinct objects of interpretation. Different objects would then answer to different interpretations. Thus, multiplism would not obtain.

Now one of the grounds for pluralizing objects of interpretation might just be a divergence in the aims that the candidate interpretations address. That is, one might urge that each of the pairs of interpretations (say, in the Kiefer case or in the soteriologies case) is admissible if they address different aims. That is, the celebratory interpretation *taken for elucidation* might be admissible and the exorcist interpretation *taken for edification* (or vice versa) might be admissible. Or, Hinduism *taken for elucidation* might be admissible and Buddhism *taken for edification* (or vice versa) might be admissible. Under these conditions both interpretations of each pair might be admissible. But when each in the pair is taken to pursue different aims, *they would no longer be incongruent with each other.* Under these conditions, multiplism would not obtain at all. Multiplism would be served only when pertinent pairs of interpretations address a given aim. Accordingly, the multiple-aims argument does not mandate multiplism. Before the operative aims are disentangled, it only looks as if the multiple-aims argument supports multiplism. So, the argument that apparently incongruent interpretations may be admissible if they pursue different aim turns out to be self-defeating. For if they did pursue different aims they would no longer be incongruent. And such incongruence is necessary for multiplism.

In the next chapter I offer a fuller account of Hinduism and Buddhism to further illustrate the copresence and the relation between the aims of elucidation and edification. That account will also reflect the limits of rightness in such soteriological cases.

NOTES

1. Robert Stecker, *Artworks: Definition, Meaning, Value* (University Park: Pennsylvania State University Press, 1997), 115.

2. Stecker, *Artworks,* 180.

3. Rafael Lopez-Pedraza, *Anselm Kiefer: 'After the Catastrophe'* (London: Thames and Hudson, 1996), 13–16.

4. Lopez-Pedraza, *Anselm Kiefer,* 78.

5. Lopez-Pedraza, *Anselm Kiefer,* 46.

6. Tenzin Gyatso, the Fourteenth Dalai Lama, *Kindness, Clarity, and Insight* (Ithaca, N.Y.: Snow Lion, 1984), 117.

7. Stecker, *Artworks,* 243.

8. Morris Weitz, "The Role of Theory in Aesthetics," in ed. Joseph Margolis, *Philosophy Looks at the Arts* (Philadelphia: Temple University Press, 1978), 125.

9. Weitz, "The Role of Theory in Aesthetics," 131.

10. Weitz, "The Role of Theory in Aesthetics," 126.

11. Stecker, *Artworks,* 243.

Chapter Twelve

Two Soteriologies

The example of the relation between Hinduism and Buddhism is especially apt for illustrating the relation between the aims of elucidation and edification. In this chapter I offer a synoptic treatment of Hinduism and Buddhism.[1]

Each of these interpretations aims to elucidate the "nature of things." At the same time each aims to provide a path for edification, more specifically, for realization or emancipation. In pursuit of the aim of elucidation, the question arises whether Hinduism and Buddhism address the same thing, that is, whether they might constitute a multiplist condition. If they address different things an innocuous pluralism would obtain. One might hold that the Hindu idea of Oneness, the Cosmic Self or Atma, seeks to elucidate the same thing as the Buddhist idea of Emptiness or Anatma attempts to elucidate. If so, and if both the Hindu and Buddhist views are admissible, a multiplist condition might obtain. On the other hand, one might hold, as the Dalai Lama and other Buddhists do, that Oneness and Emptiness do not address the same thing. They attempt to elucidate different things. This latter construal would amount to a pluralist condition, for different interpretations would address different things.

Here the question arises of the individuation of that which is interpreted. It is natural to individuate between one or another painting, say, but the situation is different for the "nature of things" in general. For the "nature of things" here is not individuable as one thing rather than another. If it makes no sense to say that the "nature of things" is one thing, then the contest between singularism and multiplism cannot arise with respect to it. Both singularism and multiplism assume that pertinent interpretations address the *same* individuable object of interpretation. If talk of a one–one or a one–many match between the nature of things in general and its interpretation(s) amounts to a conceptual confusion, talk of singularism or multiplism would be misplaced. If it makes no sense to say that what the Hindu and the Buddhist are pointing toward is itself identifiable as numerically one—and for

123

different reasons they assert as much—then a necessary condition for either a one–one or a one–many match between object of interpretation and interpretation(s) could not obtain. Such cases would be beyond the scope of either singularism or multiplism. They would be beyond the *limits of rightness.* That would not mean, though, that talk of the nature of things in general could not be interesting, illuminating, or mythically functional.

My Hindu informants tell me that the Hindu and the Buddhist address a common thing and that the Buddhist interpretation of it is wrong. On the other hand, my Buddhist informants tell me that, while it may first appear that the Hindu and the Buddhist address a common thing, they are not really talking about the same thing. So, since the Hindu and the Buddhist disagree about whether they are talking about the same thing, they disagree about whether they disagree.

The situation is further complicated by the fact that, on their own accounts, from the point of view of a fully realized state nothing substantive can be said about what they address themselves to. Neither can affirm that they agree or disagree. In a fully realized state, neither singularism nor multiplism could be said to obtain. There the *question* of ideal admissibility could not arise. So the very question of interpretive admissibility can arise only relative to the soteriological place of the inquirer, and at that it can arise only at a "relative" or "conventional" level. Here is another *limit of rightness.*

With these preliminary remarks in mind, let us now look more closely at Hinduism and Buddhism. Keep in mind that the following account is something of an idealization for purposes of illuminating concerns of this essay. Also, there are many different Hindu and Buddhist schools, some of which disagree with one or another about such characterizations as offered here. As I said, the operative Hindu view follows in the Vedant tradition of Shankaracharya, Vivekananda, and Swami Shyam. And the Buddhist view follows in the tradition of the Prasangika Madhyamaka Consequentialist School of Tibetan Buddhism.

HINDUISM

To start with, the Hindu holds that Oneness, Atma, the Cosmic Self or the Cosmic "I," is the Absolute or Ultimate. Oneness is taken to be "pure Consciousness" or "pure Awareness." Oneness is infinite. Since there is no limit to what there is, the questions, "What preceded the world?" or "What is beyond the world?" cannot arise. So there could be no creator God who precedes or stands apart from what there is. Divinity is immanent and not transcendent. Further, Oneness is not a number, and it is not a collection of parts. So, to say that "All is One" is to say that nothing stands alone, independent of the whole. Everything depends upon everything else. The One is the indivisible whole. And, despite efforts such as the present account, Oneness finally cannot be captured by language, for language is inherently dualistic.

The elucidatory aim of Hinduism, to make sense of what there is, is coupled with its edificatory aim of providing a path toward realization or emancipation. One can come to understand that all is One, that one is a manifest aspect of the One, and meditate to overcome the dualisms that are the sources of mental afflictions. Such an overcoming is thought to allow one to become realized in bliss. Becoming at-one with Oneness involves overcoming the possessive ego-self. Correspondingly, the Hindu's mantra, "Thou Art That," or "I Am Immortal, I Am Blissful," is voiced in the name of the Cosmic "I." And by identifying one's limited self with the Cosmic Self in this way, one's movement toward realization is facilitated. In this way, elucidation gives rise to edification.

The above mentioned mantras might first appear to be blasphemous, for it might appear that the utterer presumptuously assumes the position of the One. Yet the mantras are taken as aids to reclaim the original identity of all with the One. Their enunciations are taken as vehicles for recalling that one is in union with, or one *is,* Oneness. In full realization one speaks in the name of the One, for one is Oneness. So seen, there is no blasphemy. But if it were one's egoistic self that were speaking, perhaps in a moment of self-aggrandizement rather than overcoming the ego-self, the mantras would be falsely and blasphemously uttered. Yet once it were understood that it is not the egoistic "I" that speaks but the infinite "I" that does so, there would be no blasphemy. On the contrary, from the point of view of the infinite "I," it would be blasphemous to deny that one is immortal. The Hindu affirms that if one meditates on the immortal and the blissful and one utters such mantras, one's possessive self changes. In so meditating one comes to realize that one is immortal and becomes blissful. In this way, the elucidatory aim is symbiotically tied to the edificatory or emancipatory aim.

But why should one seek to overcome one's possessive ego-self? The Hindu answers that the egoistic mentality, which is inherently dualistic, gives rise to mental afflictions connected with possessiveness, including greed, anger, jealousy, malice, and the like. The prescription for overcoming mental afflictions involves changing one's ego-centered nature. The change in one's ego-centered nature involves a recollection of one's true original nature. The change involves reclaiming the identity of the limited ego's original self. It is the cosmic original Self. Notice that, upon having overcome the ego-self, it can no longer be for the sake of the ego-self that mental afflictions will have become overcome. That initial ego-self that "desired" realization will have been transformed.

Self-realization of Oneness transcends subject–object duality. From that place nothing can be said. Yet duality is inherent in critical discourse. It is necessary for elucidation. So when one "understands" one's self in terms of language, where subject is opposed to object, such understanding can be only approximate.

The idea that one might "experience" overcoming the duality between subject and object is misleading, for the very idea of "experience" itself implicates duality. One conventionally thinks of someone experiencing something where there is an experiencer and an object that is experienced. But if there is a genuine overcoming of the duality between subject and object the very idea of experiencing drops out.

Correspondingly, when in a conventional sense one speaks of "realizing" oneself it might be thought that there is a realizer who realizes something, where, again, there is a subject–object dualism. But the point of realization is precisely to overcome just such a subject–object dualism. In realization the conventional idea of realization drops out. In realization the conventional subject–object duality drops out. In Oneness there is no separation between subject and object. In such a state, consciousness is not consciousness *of* something separate from itself. Indeed, Oneness is understood to be pure consciousness without a separate object of consciousness. Put still otherwise, there is knowingness without a separate knower. This knowingness is the great Cosmic "I," the Self, the Atma.

Accordingly, in realization it would be misleading to say that one becomes identified with the One, for identification still presupposes a dualism, where an individual has a certain sort of relationship with the One, where the relation is dyadic and therefore dualistic. In the end, the realization of Oneness cannot be a dualistic *relation*. Rather, the individual and the One are in union. As well, if "embodiment" were understood in a dualistic way, it would be misleading also to say that the One is "embodied" in individuals. Generally, then, while in conventional moments one might be tempted to speak in terms of "experience," "realization," "identification," or "embodiment" with their usual dualistic connotations, doing so runs counter to the sought-after overcoming of the dualisms precisely necessary for realization. For the Hindu, the paradoxes generated by speaking in conventional ways attests to the inherent dualism of conventional language. As regards realization, the resources of language give out.

Let us draw out some consequences of the Hindu view, at least at the conventional or relative level, as the Hindu would have it. Since at the conventional level any property is distinguished by its negation, and since in Oneness there is no duality, Oneness cannot be distinguished from anything else. This, in turn, means that, at the absolute level, the law of noncontradiction does not apply, for the law of noncontradiction holds that a thing cannot both be and not be itself at the same time and in the same respect. If that to which the law might apply has no respects (or properties or features) then the law cannot apply to it. Ultimately, the One admits of no properties, for it is nondualistic. At the ultimate level individuating properties cannot apply.

Further, the One's having no properties at the absolute level means that the property of *existence* cannot be predicated of it, for that property—if it is one—also implicates its negation of nonexistence. But, at the conventional level one might object that the One's having no properties *is* a property, if, that is, negative properties count as properties. Further, if one grants that having no properties is itself a property, then the initial formulation of the One in these terms could not even get off the ground.

Here is a further paradox. If at the absolute level the One has no properties, it cannot have the property of being the goal of liberation, for example, for having the goal of liberation is still dualistic. It contrasts with its negation, another goal or no goal. Only at the conventional level can it "falsely" or approximately be said what is aimed at. Further, at the ultimate level it cannot be said that Oneness is knowingness, for example, because knowingness is a property in contrast with nonknowingness, and so on. At the ultimate level all predication drops out. At the ultimate level, even such mantras as "Thou Art That" drop out.

For the Hindu, it is only at the conventional level that one might distinguish the aims of elucidation and edification. It is only at the conventional level that the question could be raised whether singularism or multiplism might arise. Generally, then, being mindful of the soteriological place from which we make this assertion, we may say that the Hindu's mantra, "Thou Art That," serves to elucidate the nature of things and it serves to edify by facilitating one's journey toward realization.

BUDDHISM

Now consider how the Buddhist's view serves both elucidatory and edificatory aims. Central to Buddhism is the doctrine of emptiness. It urges that there is no inherent existence. This does not mean that all is void or that all is an abyss. Buddhism is not nihilistic. It means, rather, that there is nothing that exists *inherently*. And just as there is no inherent individual possessive ego-self, there is no inherent Cosmic Self or Cosmic "I," or Atman. So, when one overcomes one's possessive ego-self one does not become at-one with a Cosmic "I" or Self. One achieves liberation from suffering and mental affliction when one meditates on and realizes emptiness.

Buddhism holds, further, that all things *dependently arise* from causes and conditions. There is no autonomous or atomic individual. Nothing exists from "its own side." Consequently, there can be no first cause, for that would be an autonomous existent that would arise independently of interdependent and caused conditions. What delineates one individual from another are not inherently definable essences but conventions. There is no substantive "I."

Lobsang Gyatso says:

> Whatever depends on causes and conditions is empty of inherent existence. . . .
> The Middle Way Consequentialists argue that all phenomena arise in depend-
> ence on causes and conditions and are therefore not established from their own
> side, do not exist by way of their own identity and are not inherently existent. .
> . . Christians accept that the world was created by God, while God's existence
> on the other hand is not under the influence of causes and conditions. If the cre-
> ation of God is discussed at all the answer would seem to be that he is eternal or
> self-created. . . . Tracing the causes backwards they arrive at a primordial being
> who stands outside the realm of change, an ultimate source from which all other
> phenomena derive their truly or inherently existent natures.[2]

The Buddhist holds that there are no phenomena that exist inherently. This
view contrasts with the Hindu view that Atma exists inherently, intrinsically,
uncaused, or unconditioned. Buddhism affirms that all things are caused and
conditioned and are empty of inherent existence.

Of dependent arising, the Dalai Lama says:

> All Buddhist systems assert . . . dependent arising. One meaning of the doctrine
> of dependent arising is that all impermanent things—products or things that are
> made—arise in dependence upon an aggregation of causes and conditions; there-
> fore they arise dependently. The second meaning of dependent-arising, however,
> is that phenomena are designated, or come into being, in dependence upon the
> collection of their own parts. The breaking down of phenomena by scientists into
> extremely small particles serves to support this doctrine that phenomena are des-
> ignated in dependence upon a collection of parts, these parts being their minute
> particles. A third meaning of dependent-arising is that phenomena only nomi-
> nally exist. This means that phenomena do not exist in and of themselves objec-
> tively but depend upon subjective designation for their existence. When it is said
> that phenomena exist or are designated in dependence upon conceptual con-
> sciousness—which designates them as this or that—we are not saying that there
> are no objects external to the consciousnesses perceiving them as is asserted in
> the Mind Only system. There it is said that phenomena are only mental appear-
> ances, but again not that forms and so forth do not exist, rather that they do not
> exist as external objects—objects external in entity to the mind. In this way the
> meaning of dependent-arising becomes deeper and deeper in these three inter-
> pretations.[3]

A particular thing, a cup for example, may appear to exist inherently, but the
cup is a cup because humans impute it as a cup. It can be used to drink from.
That does not mean that it embodies a form of cupness in virtue of which it
is a cup. It is a cup because humans assign a function to it. There is nothing
inherently in it that makes it a cup. In this way it is conditioned to be a cup.
It is not a cup "from its own side." And this is true of all particular things.

Consider another example. A paper note does not inherently have a value of a hundred dollars "from its own side." Rather, it has to fit into a system that imputes value. To be authentic it must have a certain watermark, a type of paper, print, number, and so on issued by a certain sort of institution within a legitimate monetary system. Yet not just anything can be imputed for an authentication.

Yet to deny that there is inherent existence is not to deny that there are real existents. Everything that one ordinarily experiences remains real. It just is not inherently real. Under these conditions one can still discriminate between the true and the false, or between the real and the imaginary. If one sees water in the cup and touches its wetness, for example, one may conclude that it is real and not illusory. It can sustain more and more tests of experience. It can sustain a longer story.

The principle of emptiness extends, most importantly, to the emptiness of the self. The Dalai Lama says:

> In this highest of systems, as in the others, there is an assertion of selflessness, but this does not mean that there is no self at all. In the Middle Way Consequence School it means that when we search to find the kind of self that appears to our minds so concretely, we cannot find it. Such a self is analytically unfindable. Analytic findability is called "inherent existence"; thus, when the Middle Way Consequence School speaks of selflessness, they are referring to this lack of inherent existence. However, they do assert that there is a self, or I, or person that is designated in dependence upon mind and body.[4]

When one first begins to gain an understanding of emptiness, it appears that there is a subject that one understands and an object, emptiness, that is being understood. Yet as one gains a direct understanding or realization of emptiness, the appearance of there being a subject viewing an object dissipates. This is not to say that there is still no distinction between subject and object. It is to say, rather, that no such appearance is presented to the knower who directly realizes emptiness. For one who realizes emptiness directly there is no appearance of the subject and object duality. Yet it is at the conventional level that it is said that the distinction between subject and object does not appear. We may say that the elucidatory activity has been effected by one's edificatory place.

The Buddhist distinguishes between conventional truth and ultimate truth. One type of mind deals with conventional things and with conventional truths. The other type of mind deals with the ultimate nature of things. It is that latter mind that comes to understand emptiness. Now, the very distinction between these minds is drawn by the conventional mind. Saying that these minds are different involves a conventional judgment. Yet when one reaches Buddhahood, the ultimate and the conventional appear simultaneously.

To illustrate the distinction between conventional and ultimate mentalities the Buddhist offers the metaphor of a lit candle on a table. When a strong overhead electric light is off, and when one does not look directly at the candle's flame, one can tell that the light of the room is coming from the candle. Then, when one turns on the electric light one can no longer discern the light of the candle, since the electric light is so powerful. The light illuminated by the candle seems to have disappeared. The Buddhist likens the direct realization of emptiness to the electric light, and he likens the understanding of conventional appearances to the light illuminated by the candle. It is not as though conventional appearances are not there when one realizes emptiness. Rather, the realization or the understanding of emptiness is so powerful that conventional appearances recede. While one cannot see the light of the candle when the electric light is on, one can reason that the candle's light is still there somewhere. It does not just disappear when the electric light goes on and reappear when the electric light is turned off.

In the conventional understanding of a table, say, one who understands has a sense of a subject and a sense of a distance between a subject and an object. When there is a direct understanding of emptiness one gets rid of the apparent distinction between the subject and object. The sense of the difference between the subject and the object decreases until, when finally one realizes emptiness directly, conventional appearances disappear from the point of view of that mind. The point where the conventional understanding is surpassed, where one no longer relies on conventional understanding, is the point where one realizes emptiness directly.

The feeling of the substantive inherent "I" is the basis of all negative emotions. And that should be overcome. The Buddhist holds that the experience of emptiness directly opposes negative emotions of attachment such as pride or anger. In denying inherent existence one clings less to a false security of supposed inherent existents. When one realizes that all things, including one's own self, are empty of inherent existence one can dissipate destructive emotions or mental afflictions that arise from the false picture of inherent self-existence. One loosens one's clutches to one's self and to others. One realizes that anger, for example, and the persons or situations to whom one directs anger do not exist from their own side. Anger dissipates when one realizes that its objects do not inherently exist. One will be more at peace, even with one's enemies. As well, the Buddhist holds that when one regards the objects of love as inherently existing one characteristically becomes possessive of them. People who are enraptured of one another tend to regard each other as existing inherently. But they cannot be fixed as something that exists from their own side. According to the Buddhist, realizing emptiness changes one's possessive attitude to all things.

The Dalai Lama remarks that experiences of emptiness deepen only gradually. Moments of negation become longer and longer. Eventually one's sense of one's own organs dissolves. Although one sees, one does not see that one sees. Although one feels, one does not feel that one feels. One simply becomes absorbed in the negation. At that moment there is no sense or realization of realization. At that moment there is simply negation.

When in meditative equipoise, in the direct realization of emptiness, one cannot ask the question, "Is emptiness true?" for such a question reinserts a dualistic mentality. Yet after one returns to the conventional dualistic mentality, one can ask, "Did I truly experience emptiness?"

The Dalai Lama says:

> Thus, for the mind of a person realizing emptiness there is no sense of, "I am ascertaining emptiness," and there is no thought, "This *is* emptiness." If you had such a sense, emptiness would become distant. Nevertheless, the emptiness of inherent existence is ascertained and realized.[5]

At the time of equipoise one cannot say that one is "experiencing." But the subject–object duality still operates, and it is in virtue of that continued operation that one can, after equipoise, refer to what had happened in an experience. Put otherwise, while from the point of view of the experiencer at the time there was no separate experiencer, there *was* a distinct experiencer. At the moment of equipose the experiencer does not grasp the fact of being an experiencer. At the same time, what appears to the experiencer in equipose is the ultimate nature of things. The Buddhist likens the situation to sleep. One is not generally aware that one is asleep at the time of being asleep. Yet, when one wakes up, one can look back at that experience and recognize that one had been asleep. By so doing one is not postdictively inventing an experiencer. Rather, one was just not aware of the experiencer in the dream state.

Accordingly, in equipose, the mind is directly aware of emptiness. And that is not to deny that there is an experience. While at the moment of direct awareness of emptiness one has no sense of having an experience, afterward one can recall that one had such an experience, for there was such an experience. While the person who experiences emptiness does not then experience himself as a knowing subject, the distinction between subject and object still operates then. And it can be truly said that the person experienced emptiness.

The fact that the subject–object distinction is not known in equipoise is a matter of some intramural contention among Buddhist schools. Consequentialists hold that one can have an experience and then later become aware that one had an experience without it being the case that on the first occasion one was aware that one was experiencing something. A "lower" Buddhist school asserts that, *along with* any experience, there is a part of the mind that always experiences the experiencer. And this is necessary in order later to know that one had an experience. One can know that one had experienced something only if one originally had been aware that it was then experiencing something.

The realized state of Buddhahood is that state in which one experiences conventional and ultimate truths simultaneously. In Buddhahood one brings the two experiences together in a single mind. One sees the vase, for example, as a vase. One conventionally understands it as a particular thing. Yet simultaneously one also realizes its ultimate emptiness. The aim of Buddhist soteriology, the achievement of Buddhahood, is to bring together in a single experience the realization of conventional things and their ultimate emptiness.

Buddhism directs itself to two discernible aims. First, it aims to explain the way things are. Second, it aims toward realization or emancipation, which involves the elimination of suffering and mental affliction. Both aims are satisfied by the realization of the emptiness of inherent existence and the subsequent achievement of Buddhahood. In Buddhahood, both aims are satisfied. Notice that the ambiguity of the term "realization" points toward the pursuit of the two aims. One can realize something in the elucidatory sense that such and such is the case. And one can realize something in the sense that one has achieved something, in this case emancipation or liberation. Both senses operate in the Buddhist view. It is this ambiguity that signals the dual aims of the Buddhist soteriology.

HINDUISM AND BUDDHISM COMPARED

Very broadly, we may compare the Hindu and the Buddhist views by remarking on their views about individuals in relation to death. By affirming that individuals are the manifest aspects of the One, the Hindu denies that the individual is the inherent autonomous being that might otherwise be thought to die. And by affirming that all is empty of inherent existence, the Buddhist denies that anything is the inherent being that might otherwise be thought to die. Both agree that the individual is no inherent existent and thus it does not die as one might think an inherent autonomous individual might die.

While Hinduism holds that in the end all things are manifest aspects of the cosmic inherent existent, the Atma, Buddhism holds that all things lack inherent existence, including ordinary objects and the self, whether individual or cosmic. Now, it appears that the Hindu and the Buddhist are talking about "the way things are," only disagreeing about how it should be understood. But it is unclear whether they are really talking about the same thing. Their accounts implicate different conceptions of "the way things are" to start with. So at the level of elucidation, it is contentious as to whether they disagree. The Buddhist urges that with refined specification of the understanding of the nature of things, it becomes clear that adherents of each tradition address themselves to different objects of interpretation. In contrast, the Hindu holds that with refined specification of the understanding of things it becomes clear that adherents of each tradition address themselves to a common object of interpretation, but that the Buddhist is wrong.

Generally speaking, Hinduism and Buddhism aim for "similar" things: elucidation of the way things are and the attainment of liberation that eliminates suffering. But the Buddhist urges that as the general aims as first described become focused and refined, it becomes apparent that the aims are not the same. Consequently, as common ground dwindles, the possibility of competition dissipates. The Hindu and the Buddhist share an interim aim, that of overcoming duality. Yet, while the Buddhist understands the overcoming of duality in terms of emptiness, the Hindu understands the overcoming of duality in terms of at-Oneness.

The Dalai Lama provides the analogy of an academic curriculum to illustrate the growing divergence. In secondary school all students share more or less the same course of study: reading, writing, and arithmetic. Analogously, all religions share the aim of encouraging people to be good, contributing, and caring members of their community. In turn, at the more advanced university level, people specialize and follow different areas of interest. They pursue more specified aims. Analogously, different religions are interested in pursuing different more specialized aims.

While the Hindu and the Buddhist disagree that in the end they are talking about the same thing, and while they disagree about what constitutes realization, they agree that one cannot *say* what the ultimate reality is or that it has been captured. So it remains an open question whether they actually are talking about the same thing.

The Hindu and the Buddhist agree that, insofar as it is dualistic, language prohibits either from describing their *ultimate* object of concern. And they agree that in realization, subject–object dualities should be overcome, for such dualities contribute to mental afflictions and inhibit full liberation. Overcoming the dualities of language is part and parcel of both soteriologies. It is only at the *relative* or the *conventional* level that the Hindu and the Buddhist can talk about whether they are talking about the same thing or whether they aim at the same thing. Ultimately, they cannot *say* whether they are talking about the same thing or whether they are aiming at the same thing. Ultimately, the object of concern is inexpressible. So, at the limit, the question whether the Hindu and the Buddhist address the same thing or aim at the same thing is undecidable. The very question of the commonality of their concerns can be posed at a relative or conventional stage only where language still applies. Thus, the very question whether this pair of interpretations constitutes a singularist or a multiplist condition can arise only at the relative or conventional level, and even then only approximately.

At the conventional or relative level one might affirm that the Hindu and Buddhist *objects* of interpretation should be aggregated or pluralized, or that the Hindu and Buddhist *interpretations* themselves should be aggregated or pluralized. But whatever considerations might be adduced for these strategies, in light of their respective views about ineffability, at the ultimate level such a discussion would be inapplicable. At the ultimate level, the very question of admissibility or rightness cannot arise.

For Hinduism and Buddhism, the questions of this book can arise only at the conventional or relative level. That is, the question of the relation between singularism and multiplism to various ontologies, the question of the aims of interpretation, and the question of the admissibility of a single or multiple life paths can be taken up only at a certain stage in one's soteriological development. At the ultimate level—where, on different grounds, the distinction between subject and object is overcome, where the distinction between otherwise contending interpretations is overcome, where the distinction between otherwise contending aims is overcome—the questions of the ideals and aims of interpretation do not arise. The limits of rightness will have been reached.

Yet, to recall a remark made in the last chapter, we may note that at the relative level, if Hinduism is taken to aim toward elucidation and Buddhism is taken to aim toward edification (or vice versa), there would be no pertinent opposition between these interpretations. Correspondingly, since such opposition between interpretations is necessary for the multiplist condition to obtain, under these conditions multiplism would not obtain. Rather, an innocuous pluralism would. The fact that multiple aims may be pursued does not mandate multiplism.

NOTES

1. My account of Hinduism and Buddhism is a reconstruction for purposes of highlighting the issues of concern to this essay. It does not presume to be a comprehensive account of either, nor does it indicate the intramural differences between schools of thought within each of these traditions. I pick these versions of each tradition for purposes of generating particular questions about interpretation and its possible aims. In so doing I claim no comprehensiveness. The characterization of the Hindu view reflects the Vedant orientation of Adi Shankaracharya, Swami Vivekananda, and their disciple, Swami Shyam. It is informed by interviews with Swami Shyam himself at the International Meditation Institute in Kullu, India, 1991–1999. It is further informed by discussions with Professor Srinivasa Rao of the University of Bangalore, India, in 1996. In turn, the characterization of the Buddhist view reflects the Prasangika Madhyamaka consequentialist orientation, notwithstanding differences between it and other Buddhist schools. It is informed by private interviews with His Holiness the Dalai Lama in Dharamsala in 1992 and 1995. It is also informed by interviews in 1995 and 1996 with Ven. Lobsang Gyatso, Director of the Institute for Buddhist Dialectics in Dharamsala (until his untimely death in 1998). The characterization arises further from interviews in 1997 and 1999 with Ven. Samdhong Rinpoché and Ven. Ngawang Samten at the Institute of Higher Tibetan Buddhist Studies in Sarnath, India. Finally, Professor Jitendra Mohanty has provided guidance. I am deeply grateful to all of these thinkers.

2. Lobsang Gyatso, *The Harmony of Emptiness and Dependent-Arising* (Dharamsala: Library of Tibetan Works and Archives, 1992), 45–46.

3. Tenzin Gyatso, the Fourteenth Dalai Lama, *Kindness, Clarity, and Insight* (Ithaca, N.Y.: Snow Lion, 1984), 55–56.

4. Gyatso, *Kindness, Clarity, and Insight,* 55.

5. Gyatso, *Kindness, Clarity, and Insight*, 42.

Chapter Thirteen

Life Paths and Projects

I have assumed an antiessentialism in an orthodox sense. It is time to make that orthodox sense more explicit. In so doing I shall consider two treatments of human nature, those of Martha Nussbaum and David Norton. Both of them are concerned with the admissibility of multiple "life paths," and they are so in terms of different construals of essentialism. While I do not resist Nussbuam's heterodox essentialism, I resist Norton's orthodox essentialism. Finally, I shall offer an account that rejects an orthodox essentialist understanding of what Norton thematizes as "inner necessity."

ESSENTIALISM

I take essentialism in its orthodox sense to hold that a thing is what it is inherently and invariantly, irrespective of its relation to other things or interests. Popper formulates it this way.

> The doctrine which I have called 'essentialism' amounts to the view that science must seek ultimate explanations in terms of essences: if we can explain the behaviour of a thing in terms of its essence—of its essential properties—then no further question can be raised, and none need be raised (except perhaps the theological question of the Creator of essences).[1]

Popper continues:

> I reject all *what-is questions*: questions asking what a thing is, what is its essence, or its true nature. For we must give up the view, characteristic of essentialism, that in every single thing there is an essence, an inherent nature or principle (such as the spirit of wine in wine), which necessarily causes it to be what it is, and thus to act as it does. This animistic view explains nothing; but it

137

has led essentialists . . . to shun relational properties . . . and to believe, on grounds felt to be a priori valid, that a satisfactory explanation must be in terms of inherent properties (as opposed to relational properties). . . . We must give up the view, closely associated with animism . . . that it is the essential properties inherent *in each individual or singular thing* which may be appealed to as the explanation of this thing's behaviour. For this view completely fails to throw any light whatever on the question why different things should behave in like manner. If it is said, 'because their essences are alike,' the new question arises: *why should there not be as many different essences as there are different things?*[2]

In the human realm, Bimal Matilal observes that a universalist understanding of human needs should not be cast in essentialist terms. As noted in chapter 1, Matilal says:

Noticing that a culture resists drastic changes in norms, we may unconsciously be driven to a belief in the immutability of the norms or the central core of a culture — a belief that may well amount to a sort of "essentialism." . . . Once we give up the "essentialist's" dogma, we would find it natural to talk about not mutilation or destruction but mutation and change.[3]

Immutability may be thought to obtain as much for individual persons as for cultures, and the impulse to construe both in (orthodox) essentialist terms is as tempting as it is misguided. Even if one were to agree that certain dispositions are common and universal across cultures — such as (on Matilal's account) the removal of suffering, love of justice, courage in the face of injustice, pride, shame, love of children, delight, laughter, happiness, need of affection, the cooperation of others, a place in a community, and help in trouble — their construal in terms of some "intractable human essence" is unwarranted. However common or universal one's list of dispositions, the temptation to place an orthodox essentialist construal on them should be resisted. Commonality or universality does not imply essentiality in the orthodox sense.

NUSSBAUM

In contrast to the orthodox essentialist view, Nussbaum takes her belief in a "determinate human nature" to be essentialist in a heterodox sense.[4]

Nussbaum understands her (heterodox) essentialism "as the view that human life has certain central defining features."[5] She also characterizes it as providing a "determinate account of the human being, human functioning, and human flourishing."[6] But she holds that the enumeration of what it takes to be human is empirical and not metaphysical. This distinguishes her heterodox view.

Notice that an antiessentialist of the orthodox sort could well agree with Nussbaum when she says that "those who would throw out all appeals to a determinate account of the human being, human functioning, and human flourishing are throwing away far too much—in terms even, and especially, of their compassionate ends."[7]

So much hangs on one's understanding of a "determinate account of the human being, human functioning, and human flourishing." Nussbaum nests such understanding within a broadly antirealist ontology when she says:

> implications [of attacks on metaphysical realism] are clear. If the only available (or perhaps even coherent) picture of reality is one in the derivation of which human interpretations play a part, if the only defensible conceptions of truth and knowledge hold truth and knowledge to be in certain ways dependent on human cognitive activity within history, then the hope for a pure unmediated account of our human essence as it is in itself, apart from history and interpretation, is no hope at all but a deep confusion. To cling to it as a goal is to pretend that it is possible for us to be told from outside what to be and what to do, when in reality the only answers we can ever hope to have must come, in some manner, from ourselves.[8]

Nussbaum's antirealism (or, following Putnam, her "internal realism") prompts her to characterize her essentialism as "internal essentialism," and that is meant to allow her to chart the way for a universalist "thick-though-vague" *historicized* conception of the human being. That project accords with antiessentialism in its orthodox sense.

Nussbaum presses her "internal essentialism" with the thought of defining humans in terms of necessary or essential conditions. She appreciates that within the sphere of human practices the enterprise of distinguishing essential from accidental conditions of things is altogether compatible with antiessentialism of an orthodox sort. That was the point of our saying in chapter 11 that what is intrinsic or essential to a thing or a concept is compatible with antiorthodox essentialism. Nussbaum says:

> one might accept these [antirealist] conclusions and still be [an "internal"] essentialist. One might, that is, believe that the deepest examination of human history and human cognition from within still reveals a more or less determinate account of the human being, one that divides its essential from its accidental properties.[9]

Again, one can embrace an account of more or less determinate human features without affirming that an orthodox essentialism follows. Accordingly Nussbaum says:

> I . . . propose one version of such a historically grounded empirical essentialism—which, since it takes its stand within human experience, I shall now call "internalist" essentialism.[10]

The rejection of metaphysical realism in favor of an historicized philosophy is compatible with an empirical effort to articulate the minima of what it is to be human. And it is all right to pursue such a project without the expectation that it will uncover inherent and invariant essences. Accordingly, Nussbaum is right to object to the oft-made but mistaken inference she rehearses as follows:

> Very often . . . the collapse of metaphysical realism is taken to entail not only the collapse of essentialism about the human being but a retreat into an extreme relativism, or even subjectivism, about all questions of evaluation.[11]

Nussbaum's project of providing the minima of what it is to be human seeks to capture, however vague though thick, a list of necessary and sufficient conditions. Nussbaum's apt phrase, "Thick Vague Conception," allows for a good deal of room for the diversity of local practices that may be collected under universal-though-internal terms. It allows for a multiplicity of ways of living, or for "directional multiplism," as I shall say.

Finally, Nussbaum offers her account generally to further cross-cultural attunement. She says:

> if we proceed in this way, using our imaginations, we will have in the end a theory that is not the mere projection of our own customs but is also fully international and a basis for cross-cultural attunement.
>
> The list of features that we get if we reflect in this way is, and should be, openended. . . . The list is an intuitive approximation, whose purpose is not to cut off discussion but to direct attention to certain features of importance. The list, moreover, is heterogeneous, for it contains both limits against which we press and capabilities through which we aspire.[12]

Nussbaum's heterodox essentialism amounts to a rejection of orthodox essentialism, and it allows for the open-endedness and heterogeneity of minimal human conditions.

NORTON

Norton's motivations are akin to Nussbaum's in that he allows for a multiplicity of the ways that different peoples fulfill minimal human conditions. If we define directional singularism as the view that there is one admissible way to pursue one's life path, and directional multiplism as the view that there is a multiplicity of admissible ways to pursue one's life path, both Nussbaum and Norton are directional multiplists. But unlike Nussbaum, Norton is an orthodox essentialist.

More pointedly, the contest between directional singularism and directional multiplism arises in David Norton's discussion about *inner necessity*, which he understands as a vocational calling. Norton characterizes inner necessity by citing Abraham Maslow when he says:

> Summarizing his research among self-actualizing persons, Maslow says, "In the ideal instance . . . 'I want to' coincides with 'I must.' There is a good matching of inner and outer requiredness. And the observer is then overawed by the degree of compellingness, of inexorability, of preordained destiny, necessity, and harmony that he perceives. Furthermore, the observer (as well as the person involved) feels not only that 'it has to be' but also that 'it ought to be, it is right, it is suitable, appropriate, fitting, and proper.'"[13]

While Maslow's way of characterizing inner necessity tends toward a directional singularist construal, Norton rejects directional singularism as dogmatic. Within inner necessity Norton wants to make room for directional multiplism. On the other hand, fearing that "[directional] multiplism . . . can too readily become a fair weather philosophy,"[14] Norton marries directional multiplism with innatism. The innatism is meant to constrain the range of admissible life paths. For Norton, more than one path may be admitted, but the range of possibilities is constrained by innate potentialities. Norton outlines his project this way.

> The fulcrum of my argument will be a class of propositions that I will term "directional" because they provide answers to the directional question that is posed by the inherent problematicity of human being—What kind of life shall be lived? . . . My intention is to show by extrapolation of Krausz's presentation that the epistemic condition of directional propositions is multiplist.[15]

And Norton adds:

> I will draw from Krausz on self-interpretation, but supplement his case for multiplism with a logically independent case of my own on behalf of an innatist thesis that I will defend against the prevalent "social constructionist" theory of the formation of the self.[16]

Norton's innatism turns out to be a kind of orthodox essentialism. And he understands his essentialism in metaphysical realist terms. He holds that there is more than one admissible way for one to pursue a meaningful life in accord with "who one is," and he characterizes "who one is" in terms of innate potentialities. For him, inner necessity need not issue in directional singularism, for inner necessity characteristically does not constrain the range of admissible courses of life to a limit of one. Put otherwise, Norton combines metaphysical realism, orthodox essentialism, and directional multiplism. Norton emphasizes his directional multiplism when he says:

> among culturally sanctioned courses of living (vocations, avocations, interpersonal relationships, regional lifestyles, etc.) each individual experiences as

intrinsically rewarding only a select and interrelated few. Criterial self-determination does not require more determinateness than this. In John Dewey's words, "The termini of tendencies are bands not lines, and the qualities that characterize them form a spectrum instead of being capable of distribution in separate pigeonholes." For example a person whose keenest satisfaction lies in nurturing the young can find it in parenting, teaching, counseling, mentoring young colleagues, and a variety of other courses of living.[17]

Norton's example of a person whose keenest satisfaction lies in nurturing the young is revealing. For he counts "nurturing the young" as the inner necessity that may subtend a range of varieties (parenting, teaching, counseling, mentoring, etc.). This way of counting the pertinent activities lends itself to a directional multiplism that is constrained by the more general innate potentiality of nurturing the young. But alternatively, parenting, teaching, counseling, mentoring, and so on may be counted differently. They may each be seen as distinct activities, each inner necessitated. In such a case, directional singularism rather than directional multiplism would obtain. Put otherwise, the room made for directional multiplism partly depends upon what one identifies as necessitated, either a more general category of activity or a specific activity. One might refine the categories yet again and suggest that, say, mentoring such and such a person in a given circumstance is what is inner necessitated. The identity of that which is inner necessitated is contestable. This raises the possibility of a directional pluralism (really a form of singularism) rather than directional multiplism. Norton seems to be left with the question pressed in previous chapters, namely, that of the countability of that which is necessitated.

Norton speaks of developing adolescents in decidedly realist terms when he says:

> social constructionism cannot account for the distinctive dynamics of adolescence, and in consequence cannot acknowledge adolescence as a distinctive stage of development with its special developmental work to do, namely the work of self-identification that begins in discovery of one's innate potentialities (self-discovery) and extends to progressively increasing self-knowledge interwoven with self-enactment, and is productive in adult life both of objective value and of the satisfaction of self-fulfillment that the Greeks termed *eudaimonia.*[18]

Yet it is unclear why a constructivist (or indeed a constructive realist) could not agree with Norton's assertion that adolescence is "a distinctive stage of development with its special developmental work." Rather like Nussbaum, Norton seeks universal "ideals of humanness" when he says:

> Beneath cultural variability undoubtedly may be found some common characteristics in ideals of humanness—some basic physical, cognitive, and affective

capacities. But . . . by "ideals of full humanness" I am not here introducing a de-
contextualized criterion.[19]

But unlike Nussbaum, Norton holds that the universalism of the "ideals of
humanness" leads one to an orthodox essentialism. He concedes as much
when he remarks:

The essentialism lies in my contention for a universal and definitive characteristic of human beings that is *logically prior* to culture.[20]

Norton says further that while

innate potentialities . . . must be prior to the experience of the individual and not
products of it . . . what an individual's potentialities are is only discoverable ex-
perientially and a posteriori, and their discovery is not a terminus but the opening of a path of an ongoing exploration and discovery.[21]

In contrast to Norton, here is another way of understanding the emergence
of the individual that does not assume an innatist or essentialist grounding. It
is offered by Bronwyn Davies and Rom Harré, who say:

An individual emerges through the processes of social interaction, not as a relatively fixed end product but as one who is constituted and reconstituted
through the various discursive practices in which they participate. Accordingly, who one is is always an open question with a shifting answer depending
upon the positions made available within one's own and others' discursive
practices and within those practices, the stories through which we make sense
of our and others' lives. Stories are located within a number of different discourses, and thus vary dramatically in terms of the language used, the concepts, issues, and moral judgments made relevant and the subject positions
made available within them.[22]

Davies and Harré hold that the self is fully constituted by discursive practices. That is, there is no explanatory role left for the notion of innate
essences. Davies and Harré reject the understanding of selves in terms of
fixed essences. For example, American masters saw the putative essences of
their slaves as inherently inferior, and Nazis saw the putative essences of Jews
as inherently evil. In contrast with the essentialist view, it is not that slave
owners or Nazis *misdescribed the essences* of African Americans or Jews.
Rather, no essences were there to be described.

An orthodox essentialist might think that essences are *there* to be found.
But rather than actualizing antecedent innate potentialities, antecedent potentialities are posited in light of who the person has become. It is a posit in light
of the foreknowledge of actuality. One retroactively infers the past potential
in light of the present actual. But such retrospective positing does not establish a preexistent essence of who one was to become. When telling the story

of one's own actualization, one posits a prior narrative self, but that does not entail a substantive essentialized self. That self as the subject of the story is a posit from the vantage point of the present actualized self. So understood, the subject of the story is no inherent being but is a construction of the presently told story. One postdictively postulates the self, the grammatical subject, that makes the narrative intelligible. At the same time, this does not mean that just any story will do. The natures of selves are postdictive constructs of plausibly entertained present narratives. And with an enriched narrative emerges a correspondingly enriched self.[23]

At the same time, the emergence of an individual through processes of social interaction as one who is "constituted and reconstituted through various discursive practices," as Davies and Harré say, allows that emergent individuals are real in a robust sense, rather along lines suggested by varieties of constructive realism. (See chapter 5.)

How, then, should we understand inner necessity? In what sense *is* the pursuit of certain life paths to be taken to be necessary? Here is a partial answer. The phenomenon that Norton refers to as "inner necessity" may be better understood in terms of the concept of a *project*. Accordingly, *inner necessity is the objective necessity of the movement toward closure of a project* as set within the terms of a practice. Leaving open the morality of the project in question, it is the project that sets admissible possibilities. So seen, the phrase "inner necessity" requires no obscure essences. There is no inherent "inner" here. Nor is there a necessity of an inherent self. On this view there is no need to construe inner necessity as attached to a peculiar essential feature of a self. Norton's case of adolescence would be handled by the thought that, in addition to biological considerations, adolescents have a characteristic curiosity about things and that gets more or less satisfied by trying various projects. Whatever necessities that obtain issue from those adopted projects and not from innate essences. And one "grows out" of adolescence when one learns that some projects lend themselves more than others to overriding interests. Projects get adopted and dropped in this way. In turn, taking up one project or another can be set within an ever-larger context of interests and life aims.

Correspondingly, the self develops in accord with values of its adopted projects. While one may choose projects without threat of violating some inherent, invariant, human essence, the idea of an inherent, invariant, essentialist self does not appear. And since some projects are more conducive than others to a life of well-being there is considerable room for critical discussion about which projects should or should not be taken up.

Yet one might object that this projectist approach does not do justice to the necessities by which projects are chosen or embraced. What about such testimonies of inner necessity as "I have to paint," or "I have to make music," or "I have to philosophize," or "I have to write poetry"? Or, more pointedly, what about such testimonies as, "I have to paint, make music, philosophize, or write poetr, in *this* way rather than *that* way"? The force of such "have tos" might be seen in terms of the consequences of not acting upon them. And characteristically they are cast in such terms as provided by poet Thomas Lux, who says, "If I don't write, I feel empty and lost."[24] That is, the necessity is mandated in virtue of the unacceptability of a life without "fullness and place." And that unacceptability need not be grounded in a putative essential self.

More fully, here are some examples of projects that one may put on the positive side of a ledger: writing a book, playing a musical instrument, conducting an orchestra, painting a series of artworks, making a relationship, making a home, raising a family, pursuing a career, caring for the sick or the elderly, helping to preserve a valued culture or tradition, pursuing certain edifying religious or social practices, pursuing a certain kind of life, seeking a higher value, or preserving the physical well-being of the planet. And here are some examples of projects that one might put on the negative side of a ledger: enslaving a people (American slavery), "ethnically cleansing" a territory (Kosovo), annihilating a race (Nazism), or eliminating a culture (China as regards Tibet). A project may be foisted upon one, as for example in such custodial projects as caring for an aged parent when no other caregiver is available. Or custodial projects may be collective, where one seeks to preserve one's people or culture or way of life when it is threatened.[25]

The point is that projects characteristically take on their own lives and may impose demands upon their agents. They may demand resolution whose features are emergent in the sense that such resolutions were not initially intended by their agents. A project characteristically seeks its own autonomous consummation. A painting that has been sufficiently shaped, for example, may demand of its artist that it be completed in a certain way, or within a range of admissible ways. If it is resolved in a way outside an admissible range, the nature of the project as initially conceived transforms into one of another kind.

David Lean's film "Bridge on the River Kwai" provides a case in which a project's autonomous demands overtake its agents. Interned Colonel Nicholson (played by Sir Alec Guinness), initially to turn his battalion into a disciplined group, seriously adopted the Japanese project of building a proper bridge in which his soldiers could take pride.[26] And Nicholson did so with imagination, zest, skill, and enthusiasm. This with the full knowledge that the bridge was to transport Japanese soldiers who were to kill the colonel's own fellow British soldiers. No wonder Nicholson's medical officer said to him, "What you are doing could be construed as collaborating with the enemy." No wonder the Allied forces activated Force 316 to take up the project of blowing up the project that had "overtaken" the colonel. And such a project may reflect certain values within its own terms, such as fidelity, authenticity, and integrity. Indeed, such values may also be found, for example, in Adolf Eichmann's project to exterminate all Jews and in the present Chinese government's project to destroy the Tibetan people and culture.

Generally, then, I suggest that projectist necessities better capture the "necessity" found in cases adduced of inner necessity, except that there is nothing that is essentialist or "human naturish" about projectist necessity. And, there is no inherent "inner" in inner necessity. In short, projectist necessity leaves behind the unwanted disadvantages of an innatist essentialist metaphysics. Projectist necessities better capture Abraham Maslow's thought that "In the ideal instance . . . , 'I want to' coincides with 'I must.'"[27] Certain things "must" be done as mandated by the pertinent project, all the while bracketing the question whether those values are approbatory in a moral sense. Yet *what* it is that must be done remains variously countable, leaving open whether what must be done answers to a directional singularism or to a directional multiplism.

NOTES

1. Karl R. Popper, *Popper Selections,* ed. David Miller (Princeton, N.J.: Princeton University Press, 1985), 165.

2. Popper, *Popper Selections,* 165–66.

3. Bimal Matilal, "Ethical Relativism and Confrontation of Cultures," in ed. Michael Krausz, *Relativism: Interpretation and Confrontation* (Notre Dame: Notre Dame University Press, 1989), 351.

4. Martha Nussbaum, "Human Functioning and Social Justice: In Defense of Aristotelian Essentialism," *Political Theory,* 20, 2 (May 1992), 202–46.

5. Nussbaum, "Human Functioning and Social Justice," 205.

6. Nussbaum, "Human Functioning and Social Justice," 205.

7. Nussbaum, "Human Functioning and Social Justice," 205.

8. Nussbaum, "Human Functioning and Social Justice," 207.

9. Nussbaum, "Human Functioning and Social Justice," 207.

10. Nussbaum, "Human Functioning and Social Justice," 208.

11. Nussbaum, "Human Functioning and Social Justice," 209.

12. Nussbaum, "Human Functioning and Social Justice," 216.

13. David Norton, *Imagination, Understanding, and the Virtue of Liberality* (Lanham, Md.: Rowman & Littlefield, 1996), 108.

14. Norton, *Imagination, Understanding, and the Virtue of Liberality,* 109.

15. Norton, *Imagination, Understanding, and the Virtue of Liberality,* 85.

16. Norton, *Imagination, Understanding, and the Virtue of Liberality,* 86.

17. Norton, *Imagination, Understanding, and the Virtue of Liberality,* 106.

18. Norton, *Imagination, Understanding, and the Virtue of Liberality,* 99.

19. Norton, *Imagination, Understanding, and the Virtue of Liberality,* 115.

20. Norton, *Imagination, Understanding, and the Virtue of Liberality,* 92. Emphasis added.

21. Norton, *Imagination, Understanding, and the Virtue of Liberality,* 103.

22. Bronwyn Davies and Rom Harré, "Positioning: The Discursive Production of Selves," *Journal of Theory and Social Behaviour* 20, 1 (March 1990), 46.

23. In this vein, see Mark Freeman, *Re-Writing the Self: History, Memory, and Narrative* (London: Routledge, 1993).

24. Thomas Lux, *Los Angeles Times,* page F, section E. Monday, April 10, 1995.

25. See E. M. Zemach, "Custodians," in ed. David Theo Goldberg and Michael Krausz, *Jewish Identity* (Philadelphia: Temple University Press, 1993).

26. Pierre Boulle, "Bridge on the River Kwai." Movie directed by David Lean, Sam Spiegel Productions.

27. Norton, *Imagination, Understanding, and the Virtue of Liberality,* 108.

Chapter Fourteen

Conclusion

The present essay is meant to give pause to those who uncritically hold that singularism is required of all interpretation and to those who hold that multiplism is required for interpretation of all cultural entities. While singularism may apply under certain conditions, multiplism may apply under others. And under still further conditions neither singularism nor multiplism applies. That is the point of the title of the book, *Limits of Rightness.* It also sketches parallel conditions under which directional singularism or directional multiplism or neither applies. I collect our findings as follows.

1. Commonality. Neither singularism nor multiplism applies where otherwise competing interpretations do not address a *common* object. If the object is not common or if there are no grounds to determine whether interpretations address a countable and common object, no contest between interpretations can arise.

2. Incongruence. The multiplist disallows the conjoining of interpretations that are incongruent. Although admissible, they must remain numerically distinct. This requires an account as to what incongruence is and why it should disallow the conjoining of pertinent interpretations. Margolis's suggestion, for example, that interpretations are incongruent if on a bipolar logic they would be contradictory but on a many-valued logic they are not, does not tell us what *within* a many-valued logic incongruence amounts to. A better account of incongruence may be found in the thought that pertinent interpretations exhibit opposition without exclusivity.

3. Detachability. The issue of singularism versus multiplism is logically detachable from realism, constructivism, and constructive realism. Both singularism and multiplism are compatible with realism, constructivism, and constructive realism. Constructive realisms include those of Thom, Harré, Harrison and Hanna, Wallner, Putnam, Gupta, and Margolis. None of the ontologies in this representative inventory uniquely entails either singularism or multiplism.

4. Ontologies. These ontologies offer abductive support for the hypothesis that it is *characteristic* of ontologies that they necessitate no claim about the singular or multiple interpretability of pertinent objects. Yet, while not propounding any one of the inventoried ontologies, to say that an ontology, to qualify as realist, constructivist, or constructive realist, does not entail either singularism or multiplism is not to say that one could not formulate a realist type or constructivist type or constructive realist type of ontology by freighting it so that it might entail singularism or multiplism. The point is that a realist or constructivist or constructive realist ontology need not entail singularism or multiplism.

5. Detachability and Metaphysics. The thesis that ontology is detachable from ideality does not mean that metaphysics more generally understood is irrelevant to the understanding of interpretive activity. For example, the intentionality of cultural entities—their settings in regard to rules, norms, and the like—is a broadly metaphysical consideration without which one could not countenance pertinent entities as cultural to begin with.

6. Piecemeal Approaches. A piecemeal realist with respect to objects may say that some sorts of objects answer to realism while other sorts of objects may answer to constructivism. He or she may hold that there is no reason for a realist to be a global realist. Whether or not one can maintain a piecemeal realism of this sort depends upon how conclusive one takes the so-called constructivist's reductio to be.

7. The Constructivist's Reductio of Realism. According to the constructivist any attempt to drive a conceptual wedge between objects as such and objects as represented will fail, for any described object as such will be a represented object. And any represented object is nested in a symbol system of some kind or other. This is inescapable. Nothing intelligible can be said about the world independent of world-versions. This *constructivist's reductio* (of realism) tends toward the conclusion that constructivism must be global and that realism cannot be injected in a piecemeal way. The conclusivity of the constructivist's reductio in a piecemeal or a global way remains open.

8. Constructive Realism and the Constructivist's Reductio. Realist and constructivist elements may be combined in at least three ways, that is, according to (a) objects, (b) properties, or (c) levels of discourse, for example, at the first or second order. The first two ways appear to be especially vulnerable to the constructivist's reductio.

9. Second-Order Constructive Realism. A second-order constructive realist holds that any distinction between the real and the constructed at the first order should be subtended under a second-order constructivism. He or she holds that the distinction between practice-independence and practice-dependence (or representation-independence and representation-dependence) is itself constructed at the second order. At that second order the distinction is representation-dependent or practice-dependent. This still allows the first-order distinction between the real and the constructed.

10. Internal and External Constructive Realisms. Varieties of second-order constructive realism hold that *real objects* are constructed. Yet they disagree as to whether there is "materia" that precedes the symbol systems that construct and nest real objects. While *internal* constructive realists deny that there is such materia, *external* constructive realists affirm that there is. The internal constructive realist holds that there can be no appeal to anything that precedes a symbol system. The external constructive realist holds that, although it cannot be countenanced as embodying real objects, some presystematic "materia" needs to be appealed to in order to account for the construction of real objects. While the external constructive realist concedes that real objects are not outside symbol systems (or that one cannot make sense of the claim that real objects are outside symbol systems), this concession does not prohibit one's positing that there is something *there* outside of symbol systems that constitutes the "materia" from which real objects are constituted within symbol systems.

11. Margolis's Constructive Realism. Insofar as he holds that the distinction between natural and cultural objects is itself subtended under a second-order constructivism, we may count Margolis as an internal constructive realist. For him there is no materia beyond the range of what is constructed. Such is his thesis of the historied nature of all objects and their interpretations.

12. Thom's Three Tiers. Thom holds that, indirectly, the "further object" answers to the interpretations of the objects-as-represented. The further object is the "materia" out of which the object-as-represented is constructed. Yet pluralism rather than multiplism obtains directly between the interpretations and the object as represented. But if the further object is not individuable (that is, countable and common) neither singularism nor multiplism can apply with respect to it. Without individuation of the further object, interpretations cannot compete. Thom assumes that the further object is one and only one and that it affords and is represented by objects as represented. But he provides no grounds for individuating further objects.

13. Harré's Phenomena. Harré holds that it is "world-stuff" that, in indissoluble union with apparatus, affords "phenomena" with empirical content that in turn may answer to various interpretations. The "world-stuff" is not individuable as constituting discrete "real objects." It is not countable. Thus one cannot say that it, singularly, is that which interpretations are about. Even were one to say that *indirectly* interpretations are about the world-stuff, its singularity could not be assumed. It is not countable. At this level neither singularism nor multiplism can apply. Further, the claim that phenomena obtain in world-apparatus complexes is *logically distinct* from the rider of alternativity. That is, the rider of alternativity is neutral with respect to the question of whether it addresses one and the same object of interpretation. A singularist might agree that phenomena reside in world-apparatus complexes and still

assert that there is one and only one admissible apparatus yhat should be coupled with the world-stuff.

14. Harrison and Hanna's Embedded World. Harrison and Hanna affirm that objects of reference ineliminably are objects of human invention. They are already presented as something that is embedded in practice, one whose features and aspects have been singled out for presentation in the way they have. Accordingly, the very idea of a practice-independent entity can have no adequational role. The embedded world may well perform all the usual functions of adequacy, including those of sorting between true and false distributive judgments. Yet it does not follow that there are many practice-embedded worlds. That there is an alternativity of them is an independent claim.

15. Wallner's Environment. Wallner takes *environment* to precede the order of constructed real objects. For him, Reality is interpretation-dependent, but this does not entail idealism. Scientific practice, for example, is not about a practice-independent world. It is about a "microworld" that is constructed. While scientific practice is about Reality, Reality is defined in terms of the microworld and not a practice-independent order. Singularism or multiplism may obtain between interpretation(s) and scientific object(s). But if interpretations were taken to be not about scientific objects but about something beyond them—that is, about environment—neither singularism nor multiplism could arise there. Wallner's notion of environment remains undifferentiated, without the identity conditions required for the environment to answer to either singularism or multiplism. For Wallner, differentiation comes only with the constitution of scientific objects.

16. Putnam's Internal Realism. Putnam's internal realism mandates neither singularism nor multiplism. While his internal realism is compatible with the alternativity of conceptual schemes, the alternativity of conceptual schemes does not entail multiplism. For it remains open whether the objects spoken *of* by the alternative conceptual schemes are the same objects. Indeed, according to Putnam, the very question whether they are of the same object makes no sense. While there may be one or more admissible interpretations of an object as understood within a given conceptual scheme, the question of whether there are one or more admissible interpretations of an object beyond interpretive schemes makes no sense.

And if, as Putnam suggests, the noumenal realm understood as a whole were to contain no countable real objects then at that level the issue of singularism versus multiplism could not arise.

17. Imputation as an Argument for Multiplism. The imputationist argument for multiplism holds that interpretive activity may impute properties to a given object of interpretation. So, given different interpretive moments, the object takes on different properties. Difficulties arise if the object so imputed ceases to be the same object that would be variously interpreted. If it is not

the same object, in the presence of otherwise competing interpretations an innocuous pluralism rather than a multiplism would obtain.

18. Nature, Number, and the Flux. One way to guarantee that with imputing interpretive activity the number of the object is not altered is, as Margolis suggests, to introduce a distinction between number and nature and to restrict imputation to nature. But it is unclear how imputation might be limited to nature in this way. For Margolis also embraces the thesis of fluxism, namely that there are no *de re* necessities and so all knowledge and its objects are in flux. In light of the thesis of the flux it is unclear how the imputability or the determinability of a cultural object's nature can *not* affect its number. And if the distinction between number and nature cannot be sustained, imputability as to nature would entail pluralizing as to number. Accordingly, even if one were to allow that a work's nature may be affected by interpretive activity, that in itself would not entail multiplism.

19. Determinability and Alternativity. The claim of imputability is logically independent of the claim of *multiple* imputability (or alternativity). The former does not entail the latter. A singularist could allow that interpretive activity alters an entity's nature, but yet affirm that there is one and only one admissible way to impute properties. A singularist could also affirm that different moments of interpretive activity yield different objects of interpretation. So seen, pluralism rather than multiplism would obtain. A singularist could accept the imputationist view without the rider of alternativity. Alternativity is compatible with either pluralism (that is, singularism) or multiplism.

20. Indeterminacy. The indeterminacy of objects of interpretation need not "invite" incongruent judgments. One might urge that a singularist condition might indeed obtain where the indeterminacy of an interpretation "matches" the indeterminacy of the object in question.

Or, one might hold that for indeterminate objects it is undecidable if they answer to either singularism or multiplism. That is, in such a case it might be best to withhold judgment as to the applicability of singularism or multiplism. The point is that multiplism is not entailed by the indeterminacy of pertinent objects.

21. Vagueness. As in the case of indeterminacy, vagueness need not issue in multiplism, for a vague object may be matched by a correspondingly vague single interpretation. Nussbaum seeks to make room for the local variability of the conditions of human being, human functioning, and human flourishing. Accordingly, Nussbaum's phrase "vague thick" is meant to allow for multiplism. But either singularism, multiplism, or undecidability is compatible with vagueness. The leeway given by vagueness does not mandate multiplism. Vagueness is also compatible with singularism or undecidability.

22. Multiple Aims of Interpretation. The multiple-aims argument for multiplism requires that more than one aim is in play, that they are not conjoinable into one, that they are opposed but not exclusive, and that the aims are

aims of interpretation. While the broad aims of elucidation and edification, for example, may be pursued simultaneously, that does not mean that they are both aims of *interpretation*. Further, the multiplicity of interpretive aims does not entail multiplism, because—where different interpretations address different aims—an innocuous pluralism rather than a multiplism obtains.

23. Aims in Symbiosis. The broad aims of elucidation and edification may be in symbiosis. However, this does not mean that they are both aims of interpretation. The intrinsic single-aim view holds that elucidation is the single aim of interpretation, and edification is no aim of interpretation. The intrinsic multiple-aims view holds that both elucidation and edification are aims of interpretation. If one understands "intrinsic" to be historically or culturally invariant, then it is vulnerable to the charge of essentialism of an orthodox kind. But "intrinsic" need not be so understood.

24. Interest-Relative Aims. If one assumes that aims are interest-relative—that is, if interpretation as such neither has nor does not have aims but takes on aims relative to interests—then the question of the aim or aims of interpretation is an empirical or anthropological one. Accordingly, the multiple aims argument for multiplism does not go through if it depends upon what aims interpretation are taken intrinsically to have, not because interpretation intrinsically has a single aim rather than a multiplicity of aims but because it has no intrinsic aims at all.

25. The Aim of Realization. Of such soteriologies as Hinduism and Buddhism, one might say that their aim is realization. And "realization" may be taken as either elucidatory or as edificatory. But one might object that such disambiguation does not respect the spirit in which the soteriologies are offered. Rather, realization is beyond either elucidation or edification. If this be so, then the aim of realization either is not an aim of interpretation, or aims of interpretation include more than elucidation and edification.

26. Essential Aims and Essentialism. To say that a practice takes a certain condition as essential by its practitioners does not amount to an essentialism that asserts a metaphysical entity, an essence, in virtue of which a thing is what it is. The remark that a certain broad aim (or aims) is essential to interpretation need not assume essentialism in the sense that a thing is what it is in virtue of an inherent and invariant essence. Knowing what interpretation is, is not apprehending some essence but being able to recognize, describe, and explain what we call "interpretation." When I say that the essential aim of interpretation is elucidation, I mean that the practice of interpretation assumes that its essential aim is elucidation. So understood, the claim that elucidation is the broad aim of interpretation (or, for that matter, the claim that another one or several other aims are the essential aims of interpretation) is a claim concerning what pertinent interpreters characteristically aim toward when interpreting. There is no inherent or invariant essence that warrants elucidation (or any other candidate) as the essential aim of interpretation.

27. Inner Necessity. Correspondingly, "inner necessity" requires no obscure essences. There is no need to construe inner necessity in terms of an inherent essentialist or annatist self. The self changes and transforms in accord with the values of its adopted projects. And one can choose projects without threat of violating an inherent, invariant, human essence. Yet there is room for critical discussion about which projects should be taken up and which should not. It is in such terms that life-plans and projects should be understood.

Such is the inventory of and commentary on our salient claims. Five general questions have motivated this work. First, what interpretive ideals should one adopt for pertinent objects of interpretation? Second, what sorts of ontological entanglements are involved in interpretive activity? Third, under what conditions do either singularism or multiplism apply? Fourth, what bearing does the aim of interpretation have on the range of ideally admissible interpretations? And fifth, how shall we understand the directionality of our life paths and projects? This book is offered to help clear the ground to pursue these questions still further.

Bibliography

Aronson, Jerrold, Rom Harré, and Eileen Cornell West, eds. *Realism Rescued.* Chicago: Open Court, 1995.

Beardsley, Monroe. "The Authority of the Text." In Monroe Beardslay, *The Possibility of Criticism.* Detroit: Wayne State University Press, 1970.

Bohr, Niels. *Essays on Atomic Physics and Human Knowledge (1958–62).* New York: Wiley, 1963.

Collingwood, R. G. *An Autobiography.* Oxford: Clarendon, 1939.

———. *Essay on Metaphysics.* Oxford: Clarendon, 1940.

Davidson, Donald. *Inquiries into Truth and Interpretation.* Oxford: Clarendon, 1984.

Davies, Bronwyn, and Rom Harré. "Positioning: The Discursive Production of Selves." *Journal of Theory and Social Behaviour,* 20, no. 1, 43–63, March 1990.

Dewey, John. *Art as Experience.* New York: Capricorn Books, 1934.

Elgin, Catherine. "The Relativity of Fact and the Objectivity of Value." In ed. Michael Krausz, *Relativism: Interpretation and Confrontation.* Notre Dame: Notre Dame University Press, 1989.

———. *Between the Absolute and the Arbitrary.* Ithaca, N.Y.: Cornell University Press, 1997.

Freeman, Mark. *Rewriting the Self: History, Memory, and Narrative.* London: Routledge, 1993.

Geertz, Clifford. "Thick Description: Toward an Interpretive Theory of Culture." In Clifford Geertz, *The Interpretation of Culture.* New York: Basic Books, 1973.

Gibson, James J. *The Senses Considered as Perceptual Systems.* Boston: Houghton Mifflin, 1966.

———. *The Ecological Approach to Visual Perception.* Hillsdale, N.J.: Lawrence Erlbaum, 1986.

Goldberg, David Theo, and Michael Krausz, eds. *Jewish Identity.* Philadelphia: Temple University Press, 1993.

Goldstein, Leon. *Historical Knowing.* Austin: University of Texas Press, 1976.

Goodman, Nelson. *Ways of Worldmaking.* Indianapolis, Ind.: Hackett, 1978.

———. "Fabrication of Facts." In ed. Jack Meiland and Michael Krausz, *Relativism: Cognitive and Moral.* Notre Dame: Notre Dame University Press, 1982.

———. "Just the Facts, Ma'am." In ed. Michael Krausz, *Relativism: Interpretation and Confrontation*. Notre Dame: Notre Dame University Press, 1989.

Gupta, Chhanda. *Realism versus Realism*. Calcutta: Allied Publishers, 1995.

Gyatso, Lobsang. *The Harmony of Emptiness and Dependent-Arising*. Dharamsala: Library of Tibetan Works and Archives, 1992.

Gyatso, Tenzin (The Fourteenth Dalai Lama). *Kindness, Clarity, and Insight*. Ithaca, N.Y.: Snow Lion, 1984.

Harré, Rom. "Is There a Basic Ontology for the Physical Sciences?" *Dialectica*, vol. 51, Fasc. 1., 16–34, 1997.

Harré, Rom, and Michael Krausz. *Varieties of Relativism*. Oxford: Basil Blackwell, 1996.

Harrison, Bernard, and Patricia Hanna. *Word and World: Reference and Linguistic Convention*. Forthcoming.

Hirsch, E. D. Jr. "In Defense of the Author." In E. D. Hirsch Jr., *Validity in Interpretation*. New Haven, Conn.: Yale University Press, 1967.

Honner, John. *The Description of Nature: Niels Bohr and the Philosophy of Quantum Physics*. Oxford: Clarendon, 1987.

Hopkins, Jeffrey. *Meditation on Emptiness*. London: Wisdom Publications, 1983.

Horgan, Terry, ed. *Vagueness*. Memphis, Tenn.: Southern Journal of Philosophy, Supplement vol. 33, University of Memphis, 1995.

Kant, Immanuel. *Critique of Pure Reason* (1781). trans. N. Kemp Smith. Königsberg, London: Macmillan, 1934.

Kimmelman, Michael. "It Was Big, It Was Fun and That's Enough." *New York Times,* July 1995, 26.

Kinzer, Stephen. "Berlin's Symbol of Hope and Agony Awaits a New Ordeal: Tinsel." *New York Times*, E5, Sunday, March 6, 1994.

Kosso, Peter. *Appearance and Reality: An Introduction to the Philosophy of Physics*. New York: Oxford University Press, 1998.

Kramer, Jane. "The Politics of Memory: Letters from Germany." *The New Yorker,* 48–65, August 14, 1995.

Krausz, Michael, ed. *Relativism: Interpretation and Confrontation*. Notre Dame: Notre Dame University Press, 1989.

———. "Crossing Cultures: Two Universalisms and Two Relativisms." In ed. Marcelo Dascal, *Cultural Relativism and Philosophy*. Leiden: E. J. Brill, 1991.

———. *Rightness and Reasons: Interpretation in Cultural Practices*. Ithaca, N.Y.: Cornell University Press, 1993.

———. "The Interpretation of Art: Comments on Multiplism and Relativity." *JTLA, Journal of the Faculty of Letters, The University of Tokyo,* Aesthetics, vol. 22, 33–42, 1997.

———. "Interpretation, Relativism, and Culture: Four Questions for Margolis." In ed. Michael Krausz and Richard Shusterman, *Interpretation, Relativism, and the Metaphysics of Culture*. Amherst, N.Y.: Humanity Press, 105–24, 1999.

———, ed. *Is There a Single Right Interpretation?* University Park: Pennsylvania State University Press, 2001.

Krausz, Michael, and Richard Shusterman, eds. *Interpretation, Relativism and the Metaphysics of Culture*. Amherst, N.Y.: Humanity Press, 1999.

Leddy, Thomas. Review of Michael Krausz, *Rightness and Reasons. Journal of Aesthetics and Art Criticism,* vol. 53, no. 2, spring, 222–25, 1995.

Lopez-Pedraza, Rafael. *Anselm Kiefer: 'After the Catastrophe.'* London: Thames and Hudson, 1996.

Margolis, Joseph. "Robust Relativism." In ed. Joseph Margolis, *Art and Philosophy: Conceptual Issues in Aesthetics.* Atlantic Highlands, N.J.: Humanities Press, 1980.

———. "The Truth about Relativism." In ed. Michael Krausz, *Relativism: Interpretation and Confrontation.* Notre Dame: Notre Dame University Press, 1989.

———. "Reinterpreting Interpretation." *Journal of Aesthetics and Art Criticism,* 47 (summer), 237–51, 1989.

———. *The Truth about Relativism.* Oxford: Basil Blackwell, 1991.

———. "Genres, Laws, Canons, Principles." In ed. Mette Hjort, *Rules and Conventions.* Baltimore: Johns Hopkins University Press, 1992.

———. *The Flux of History and the Flux of Science.* Los Angeles: University of California Press, 1993.

———. *Interpretation, Radical But Not Unruly: The New Puzzle of the Arts and History.* Berkeley: University of California Press, 1994.

———. *Historied Thought, Constructed World.* Berkeley: University of California Press, 1995.

———. "Relativism and Cultural Relativity." *JTLA, Journal of the Faculty of Letters, The University of Tokyo, Aesthetics,* vol. 22, 1–17, 1997.

———. "Reconciling Relativism and Cultural Realism." *JTLA, Journal of the Faculty of Letters, The University of Tokyo, Aesthetics,* vol. 22, 79–93, 1997.

———. *What, After All, Is a Work of Art?* University Park: Pennsylvania State University Press, 1999.

Matilal, Bimal. "Ethical Relativism and Confrontation of Cultures." In ed. Michael Krausz, *Relativism: Interpretation and Confrontation.* Notre Dame: Notre Dame University Press, 339–62, 1989.

McCormick, Peter, ed. *Starmaking: Realism, Anti-Realism, and Irrealism.* Cambridge, Mass.: MIT Press, 1996.

Meiland, Jack, and Michael Krausz, eds. *Relativism: Cognitive and Moral.* Notre Dame: Notre Dame University Press, 1982.

Mink, Louis O. "Narrative Form as a Cognitive Instrument." In ed. Robert H. Canary and Henry Kozicki, *The Writing of History: Literary Form and Historical Understanding.* Madison: University of Wisconsin Press, 147, 1978.

Mohanty, Jitendra. "Levels of Understanding 'Intentionality.'" *The Monist,* 69, October 1986.

Nehamas, Alexander. "The Postulated Author: Critical Monism as a Regulative Ideal." *Critical Inquiry,* 8 autumn, 133–49, 1981.

Norton, David. *Imagination, Understanding, and the Virtue of Liberality.* Lanham, Md.: Rowman & Littlefield, 1996.

Nussbaum, Martha. "Human Functioning and Social Justice: In Defense of Aristotelian Essentialism." *Political Theory,* vol. 20, no. 2 (May 1992), 202–46.

———. "The 'Capabilities' Advantage to Promoting Women's Human Rights." *Human Rights Dialogue* (Carnegie Council on Ethics and International Affairs), Summer 2000/Series 2, no. 3, 10–11, 13.

———. *Women and Human Development: The Capabilities Approach.* Cambridge: Cambridge University Press, 2000.

Popper, Karl R. *Objective Knowledge.* Oxford: Clarendon, 1972.

———. *Realism and the Aim of Science.* Totowa, N.J.: Rowman & Littlefield, 1983.

———. *Popper Selections,* ed. David Miller. Princeton: Princeton University Press, 1985.

Putnam, Hilary. *Reason, Truth, and History.* Cambridge: Cambridge University Press, 1981.

———. *The Many Faces of Realism.* La Salle, Ill.: Open Court, 1987.

Saltzman, Lisa. *Anselm Kiefer and Art after Auschwitz.* Cambridge: Cambridge University Press, 1999.

Schafer, Roy. "Action and Narration in Psychoanalysis." *New Literary History,* 12, 61–85, 1980.

Searle, John. *The Construction of Social Reality.* New York: Free Press, 1995.

Soffer, Gail. "Relativity, Intentionality, and the 'Puzzle' of Interpretation." In ed. Michael Krausz and Richard Shusterman, *Interpretation, Relativism, and the Metaphysics of Culture.* Amherst, N.Y.: Humanity Press, 1999.

Stecker, Robert. *Artworks: Definition, Meaning, Value.* University Park: Pennsylvania State University Press, 1997.

———. "The Constructivist's Dilemma." *Journal of Aesthetics and Art Criticism,* 55, 43–51, 1997.

Taylor, Charles. *Philosophy and the Human Sciences: Philosophical Papers,* Vol. 2. Cambridge: Cambridge University Press, 1985.

Thom, Paul. Review of Michael Krausz, *Rightness and Reasons,* Joseph Margolis, *Interpretation Radical But Not Unruly,* and Robert Stecker, "The Constructivist's Dilemma." *Literature and Aesthetics, The Journal of the Sydney Society of Literature and Aesthetics,* October 1997, 181–85.

———. *Making Sense: A Theory of Interpretation.* Lanham, Md.: Rowman & Littlefield, 2000.

———. "Rightness and Success in Interpretation." In ed. Michael Krausz, *Is There a Single Right Interpretation?* University Park: Pennsylvania State University Press, 2001.

Wallner, Fritz G. *Constructive Realism: Aspects of a New Epistemological Movement.* Vienna: Braumüller, 1994.

———. *How to Deal with Science if You Care for Other Cultures: Constructive Realism in the Intercultural World.* Vienna: Wilhelm Braumüller, 1997.

Weitz, Morris, "The Role of Theory in Aesthetics." In ed. Joseph Margolis, *Philosophy Looks at the Arts.* Philadelphia: Temple University Press, 121–31, 1978.

Williamson, Timothy. *Vagueness.* London: Routledge, 1994.

Wittgenstein, Ludwig. *Philosophical Investigations.* Oxford: Basil Blackwell, 1958.

———. *On Certainty.* Oxford: Basil Blackwell, 1969.

Zemach, E. M. "Custodians." In ed. David Theo Goldberg and Michael Krausz, *Jewish Identity.* Philadelphia: Temple University Press, 1993.

Index

activity, interpretive, 1, 2, 25, 60, 98
adequation, 67, 68, 152
admissibility, 1, 2, 8, 10
admissible interpretation, 1–2, 3, 5, 94.
    See also aims of interpretation;
    interpretation
affordance, 57, 61, 62, 63
aims of interpretation, 113–20, 153–54;
    in art, 114–15; Hinduism and
    Buddhism, 132, 133, 134; interest-
    relative, 114, 119, 154; intrinsic or
    extrinsic, 114–19, 120, 154;
    nonintrinsic, 114, 119. *See also*
    interpretation
alternative interpretations, 10, 11–12
alternativity, 15, 153; and conceptual
    relativism, 78; Harré, Rom, 59, 151;
    Harrison and Hanna, 57–58, 152;
    language, 57–58; Joseph Margolis,
    60, 87; Hilary Putnam, 59, 152;
    relative realism, 66–67
Anatma, 123. *See also* Buddhism
antiessentialism, 6, 118–19. *See also*
    essentialism
appreciation, 117
Aristotle, 88, 89
art, 29–30, 38, 95, 97, 98; aims of
    interpretation, 114–15;

antiessentialism, 118–19;
    indeterminacy of, 101–3; Anselm
    Kiefer, 21–23, 114–15, 120; Paul
    Klee, 21. *See also* cultural objects;
    history; human sciences
ascribability, of properties, 60–61, 62–63
Atma, 123, 124, 126, 127, 128, 132. *See
    also* Hinduism
autonomous individual, 127, 132

Bell, John, 52
Bohr, Niels, 60, 61, 62
Buddhism, 115–16, 120, 123–24,
    127–32, 154; compared to Hinduism,
    132–34. *See also* Hinduism

celebratory interpretations, 23–24, 114,
    120
Christo, 101–3. *See also* art
cognitive intransparency, 87–88
cognitive practices, 95, 139
Collingwood, R. G., 39–40, 103–4
commonality, 15, 25, 46, 48, 76, 106–7;
    and conceptual relativism, 78;
    singularism and multiplism, 110, 149
conceptual relativism, 77–79
conceptual schemes, 66–67, 68, 75, 77,
    152

constructive realism, 3, 31, 51, 52, 142,
144, 149–51; and alternativity, 60;
Rom Harré, 60–64; Harrison and
Hanna, 65–68; Hilary Putnam,
75–80; relative realism, 65–68;
singularism and multiplism, 57, 58,
72, 84; versions of, 56–58; Fritz
Wallner, 69–73. *See also* external
constructive realism; internal
constructive realism
constructivism, 3, 35, 42–47, 149, 150;
by level of discourse, 51, 55–56; by
object, 51–52; by properties, 51,
52–55; versus realism, 37–38, 47–49,
92–93
convergence, 9, 19, 48. *See also*
nonconvergence
countability, 12–13, 63, 84, 151; internal
realism, 76
counting, systems of, 59, 78, 79, 80
critical monism, 6–7, 9
critical pluralism, 7
cultural objects, 88, 95, 96, 97, 98; and
constructive realism, 91, 92, 93–94,
151; determinability of, 153;
indeterminacy of, 101–5;
intentionality of, 150; Joseph
Margolis on, 19–20; David Norton
on, 11–12. *See also* art; history;
human sciences

Dalai Lama (Tenzin Gyatso), 128, 129,
130, 133. *See also* Buddhism
Davies, Bronwyn, 143
dependent arising, 127–29
descriptions, 43–44, 45, 69, 70, 77; in
internal realism, 75–76; in
transcendental realism, 81, 82
designs, imputed, 20, 21. *See also*
imputationism
detachability, 3–4, 51, 149, 150
determinability, 19, 20, 25, 95, 96, 97,
153

determinacy, 39. *See also* indeterminacy
determinate human nature, 138–40
Dewey, John, 29–30
directional multiplism, 4, 140, 141–42,
146. *See also* multiplism
directional pluralism, 142. *See also*
pluralism
directional singularism, 4, 140, 141,
142, 146. *See also* singularism
dualism, 125–26, 127, 129, 130, 131,
133

edification, 2–3, 113, 114, 119, 154;
Buddhism, 129, 134; Hinduism,
115–16, 120, 123, 125, 127, 134. *See
also* aims of interpretation;
elucidation
Elgin, Catherine, 46
elucidation, 2, 113, 114–17, 119–20,
154. *See also* aims of interpretation;
edification
emancipation, 115–16, 123, 125, 132
emptiness, 123, 127, 129, 130–31, 132,
133. *See also* Buddhism
environment, 70–71, 72, 87, 152. *See
also* Wallner, Fritz
essential properties, 137, 138, 139,
143–44
essentialism, 106, 109, 117–18, 119;
heterodox, 138–40; orthodox,
137–38, 139, 140, 141, 143, 154
evidential indeterminacy, 104–5. *See
also* Soffer, Gail
exclusive interpretations, 6, 7, 24, 149
existence, 79, 80, 127–30
exorcist interpretations, 23–24, 114,
115, 120
external constructive realism, 31, 57,
58, 65, 77, 80, 84, 151; versus
internal constructive realism, 87, 93.
See also constructive realism
extrinsic aim of interpretation, 114, 115,
116, 117, 118, 119

face–vase configuration, 26, 27, 29
fallibilism, 10–11
family resemblance (of properties),
106–8
flux, 88, 89, 90, 97, 98, 153
further object, 25, 26–28, 29, 30, 32, 84,
87, 151. *See also* object as
represented; object as such; Thom,
Paul

Gibson, J. J., 60, 61, 107
global approach, 51, 52, 53, 54, 150.
See also piecemeal approach
glub, 60, 62
Goodman, Nelson, 43–44, 45–46, 47–48
Gupta, Chhanda, 79, 81–83
Gyatso, Lobsang, 128

Hamlet, 11–12
Hanna, Patricia, 57–58, 68, 84, 87, 152;
on language, 65–67
Harré, Rom, 53, 57, 58, 59, 60, 84, 87,
143, 151; on properties, 60–64; on
sameness, 107–8
Harrison, Bernard, 57–58, 68, 84, 87,
152; on language, 65–67
hermeneutic circle, 29, 30
heterodox essentialism, 138–40. *See
also* essentialism
Hinduism, 115–16, 120, 123–27, 154;
compared to Buddhism, 132–34; on
language, 125, 126; on properties,
126–27. *See also* Buddhism
historicity of thinking, 87–88
history, 41, 97; indeterminacy of, 103–5
human sciences, 91, 95, 96, 97. *See also*
art; cultural objects
humanness, 138–41, 142–43, 153. *See
also* self

idealism, 43, 150, 152
ideals, interpretive, 3, 4, 5
identity, 95, 96–97, 101

imputationism, 2, 38, 60, 108; Anselm
Kiefer, 21–23; Joseph Margolis,
20–21, 97–98; and multiplism, 152,
153; Paul Thom, 25, 26, 27. *See also*
properties (of object)
inadmissibility. *See* admissibility
incongruence, 20, 23, 96, 98; aims of
interpretation, 120; Anselm Kiefer,
works of, 21–23; multiplism, 149;
and singularism, 24, 149
indeterminacy, 1, 2, 38, 39, 98, 153;
Christo, 101–3; cultural objects,
101–5; of history, 103–5; and
singularism, 96, 105
individuation, 96, 123, 151
infallibilism. *See* fallibilism
inherent existence, 127–30, 132
inherent properties, 137, 138, 143–44
innate potentialities, 143
innatism, 141
inner necessity, 140–41, 142, 144–45,
146, 155
inputs, 77. *See also* Putnam, Hilary
inquiry, 1, 9–10; focus of, 110
intentional determinacy, 104–5. *See also*
Soffer, Gail
intentional layering, 45
intentional objects, 13–14, 45. *See also*
objects as represented
intentional properties, 94–96, 97
intentionality, 4, 13, 14, 15, 28, 45;
cultural objects, 150; Joseph
Margolis, 94–96, 97; and
singularism, 95
interaction, social, 143, 144
internal constructive realism, 31, 57, 58,
77, 84, 151; Joseph Margolis, 87,
93–94; versus external constructive
realism, 87, 93. *See also* constructive
realism; external constructive
realism
internal essentialism, 139. *See also*
essentialism; Nussbaum, Martha

internal realism, 81, 139, 152; and
conceptual relativism, 77–79; and
constructive realism, 75–76, 77; and
singularism, 83–84; versus
transcendental realism, 81–83. *See
also* constructive realism; realism
interpretation: aims of, 1,.2–3, 113–20,
132, 133, 134, 153–54; alternative,
10, 11–12; celebratory, 23–24, 114,
120; definitions of, 16; exclusive, 6,
7, 24, 149; existential, 5; exorcist,
23–24, 114, 115, 120; ideals of, 3, 4;
object of, 2, 3; opposing, 6, 23, 24,
149; three-tier structure of, 25–30,
151. *See also* multiplism; object of
interpretation; singularism
intransparency, cognitive, 87–88
intrinsic aims of interpretation, 114–19,
120, 154

Kant, Immanuel, 76, 89–90
Kiefer, Anselm, 21–23, 114–15, 120
Kimmelman, Michael, 102
Kinzer, Stephen, 101–2
Klee, Paul, 21
knowledge, 71, 77, 88, 89–90, 94, 139,
153
Kosso, Peter, 52–53
Kuhn, Thomas, 11, 12

language, 48, 57; and constructive
realism, 93; dualism of, 125, 126,
133; Harrison and Hanna on, 65–67;
Hinduism, 125, 126; Fritz Wallner
on, 69
law of noncontradiction, 24, 126
layering, intentional, 45
levels of discourse, 51, 55–56, 150
liberal multiplism, 10
liberal singularism, 10
liberation, 127, 132, 133
life path, 4, 140, 141–43, 144, 155

limits of rightness, 124, 134
Lopez-Pedraza, Rafael, 114–15

Margolis, Joseph, 19–21, 23–24, 28, 58,
60, 87–98, 149, 151; on flux, 153;
imputationism, 20–21, 97–98; on
intentionality, 94–96, 97
Maslow, Abraham, 141, 146
materia, 84, 87, 151. *See also*
environment; further object; object of
interpretation; phenomena; world-
stuff
Matilal, Bimal, 6, 138
mereology, 78, 80
metaphysical realism, 40, 75, 78, 80, 81;
and essentialism, 139, 140, 141. *See
also* realism
metaphysics, 4, 15
methodology, 40–41
microworld, 70, 71, 152. *See also*
Wallner, Fritz
mind, 129–30
Mohanty, Jitendra, 13
monism, critical, 6–7, 9
multiple-aims interpretation, 114, 116,
117, 119, 120
multiplism, 1–2, 3, 4, 9, 10, 15, 28, 29,
30, 32, 49, 149–54; aims of
interpretation, 2–3, 113, 120,
153–54; and alternativity, 59, 60,
153; Anselm Kiefer, works of, 23;
and commonality, 110, 149; and
conceptual relativism, 78–79; and
constructive realism, 84; on
convergence, 19–20; and critical
pluralism, 6–7; and determinability,
98; Hinduism and Buddhism,
123–24, 127, 133, 134; ideals of
interpretation, 5; imputationism, 2,
152; and indeterminacy, 2, 96, 105,
153; intentionality, 95; and internal
realism, 83–84; and nonconvergence,

23–24; and realism, 39; and richness, 11; strategies, 12–13; world-stuff and world apparatus, 63–64. *See also* pluralism; singularism

natural objects, 92, 151
natural sciences, 69, 95
nature, 95, 96–98, 153
necessities, 92, 98, 153; inner, 140–41, 142, 144–45, 146, 155; projectist, 144–46
Nehamas, Alexander, 5, 6–7, 8–9
nonconvergence, 19–20; and multiplism, 23–24. *See also* convergence
nonessentialism, 6. *See also* essentialism
nonintrinsic aim of interpretation. *See* aims of interpretation.
Norton, David, 11–12, 140–43, 144
noumenal world, 76–77, 152
number, 95, 96, 97, 98, 153
Nussbaum, Martha, 138–40, 153

object as represented, 25, 26, 27–28, 29, 30, 31, 37–38, 41, 48; in constructivism, 42, 150, 151; and object as such, 46, 47. *See also* intentional objects
object as such, 37–38, 41–42, 45, 150; and object as represented, 46, 47. *See also* further object
object of interpretation, 15, 25–32, 60; conceptual relativism, 78; counting, 12–13; internal realism, 75–76; multiplism, 5; nature and number of, 95, 96–98; realism versus constructivism, 51–52; relative realism, 68; singularism, 5; in transcendental realism, 81–83. *See also* constructive realism; cultural objects; intentional objects; materia; phenomena

objectivity, 14, 91, 94
Oneness, 123, 124–25, 126, 133. *See also* Hinduism
ontologies, 3–4, 15, 32, 35, 41, 49, 58, 150; and objects, 71–72
opposing interpretations, 6, 23, 24, 149
orthodox essentialism, 137–38, 139, 140, 141, 143, 154. *See also* essentialism

pan-fluxism, 98. *See also* flux
phenomena, 57, 61, 62, 63, 64, 70, 151; internal constructive realism on, 76. *See also* materia; object of interpretation
physical objects, 91, 92, 94
physical sciences, 11, 12, 52–53, 61–62, 63, 68, 91
physical stimulants, 41–42
piecemeal approach, 52, 53, 54, 92, 150
pluralism, 21, 28, 110, 151; aims of interpretation, 120, 154; and alternativity, 2, 15; and imputation, 153; and numerical identity, 98. *See also* multiplism; singularism
pluralizing objects, 12–13
Popper, Karl, 40, 41, 137–38
practice, 65–68, 152; antiessentialism on, 118; and life path, 143, 144; scientific, 69–70, 152. *See also* activity, interpretive
projects, 144–46, 155
properties (of object), 26–27, 38, 43, 60, 101; accidental, 139; ascribability of, 60–61, 62–63; changes, 105–6, 109; constructive realism, 150; essential, 137–38, 139, 143–44; family resemblance of, 106–8; Harré, Rom, 60–64; and identity, 105–9; imputationism, 152, 153; intentional, 94–96, 97; and projections, 79; realism versus constructivism, 51, 52–55

Protagoras, 88, 89
Putnam, Hilary, 59, 60, 75–80, 81, 84, 152

rationality, 7–8
real objects, 56, 57, 58, 87, 151. *See also* materia; object of interpretation; phenomena
realism, 3, 35, 37–39, 40–42, 43, 45, 46, 149, 150; arguments against, 39–40; global, 51–52; immanent, 81; by level of discourse, 55–56; metaphysical, 40, 75, 78, 80, 81, 139, 140, 141; by object, 51–52; by properties, 51, 52–55; referential, 65, 67; relative, 57; transcendental, 80, 81–83; versus constructivism, 47–49, 51–56, 92–93. *See also* constructive realism
reality, 65, 68, 81, 152; constructed, 69–72
realization, 123, 125, 126, 127, 154; Buddhism, 130, 131–32
reductio, constructionist, 52, 53, 54, 55, 150
reference, 57, 66, 96, 152
referential realism, 65, 67
relative realism, 57, 65–68. See also Hanna, Patricia; Harrison, Bernard
relativism, 97; conceptual, 77–79
representation, 28, 37, 38, 39–40, 42, 43, 45, 47–48, 150; in realism and constructivism, 51–52, 55
rightness, 1, 2, 124, 134

Saltzman, Lisa, 22
sameness and difference, 89, 107–8, 109. *See also* commonality
scientific activity, 69–70, 152
Searle, John, 38–39
second-order constructive realism, 150, 151
second-order constructivism, 55–56
second-order realism, 55–56

self, 123, 125, 129, 130, 132, 155; development of, 142–45
signs, 75–76
single-aim interpretation, 114–17, 119–20
single right interpretation. *See* singularism
singularism, 1, 2, 3, 4, 9, 10–11, 14, 32, 49, 149–54; and alternativity, 59, 60, 153; and commonality, 110, 149; and conceptual relativism, 78–79; and constructive realism, 57, 58, 84; and determinability, 98; existential version of, 5, 6–7, 8; ideals of interpretation, 5; and incongruence, 24, 149; and indeterminacy, 96, 105, 153; intentionality, 95; and internal realism, 83–84; and rationality, 7–8; and realism, 39; regulative version of, 5–6, 7, 8; strategies, 12–13; world-stuff and world apparatus, 63–64. *See also* multiplism; pluralism
social constructionism of the self, 87, 88, 90, 142
social interaction, 14, 143, 144
Soffer, Gail, 104
soteriologies. *See* Buddhism; Hinduism
Stecker, Robert, 27–28, 113, 116–17, 119
subject–object duality, 125–26, 129, 130, 131, 133
subjectivism, 43
symbiosis of subject and object, 87, 89–90, 91, 92
symbol systems, 44, 45–48, 52, 54, 55, 56, 150, 151

text, 9
Thom, Paul, 25–31, 84, 87, 151
three-tier structure of interpretation, 25–30, 151
transcendental realism, 80, 81–83. *See also* realism

truth, 139, 152
truth-claims, 90, 91
truth-conditions, 66, 67, 68
truth, conventional versus ultimate, 129–30, 131–32

universalism, 138, 139

vagueness, 153
viewpoints, 35–37
violence to practices, 6

Wallner, Fritz, 69–73, 87, 152
Weitz, Morris, 118–19
Wittgenstein, Ludwig, 42, 48, 106–7, 108, 118
word, 65, 66
world, 65, 66, 67–68
world-apparatus, 59, 60, 61, 62, 63, 64, 151
world-stuff, 59, 60, 61, 62, 63, 84, 87, 151, 152
world-version, 43, 48. *See also* representation

About the Author

Michael Krausz is the Milton C. Nahm Professor and Chair of the Department of Philosophy at Bryn Mawr College. Trained at the Universities of Toronto (Ph.D., 1969) and Oxford, Krausz has been visiting professor at Georgetown University, Oxford University, Hebrew University of Jerusalem, American University in Cairo, University of Nairobi, Indian Institute of Advanced Study, and University of Ulm, among others. He is the cofounder and former chair of the thirteen-institution Greater Philadelphia Philosophy Consortium.

In addition to *Limits of Rightness*, Krausz is the author of *Rightness and Reasons: Interpretation in Cultural Practices,* 1993) and *Varieties of Relativism*, with Rom Harré (Basil Blackwell, 1995). As well, he is editor and contributor to nine volumes on such topics as relativism, rationality, interpretation, cultural identity, metaphysics of culture, creativity, interpretation of music, and the philosophy of R. G. Collingwood. In 1997, the University of Ulm awarded Krausz the Hans Kupczyk Prize, and in 2000, the University of Delhi sponsored an international conference on his philosophical work.